TIME IS A FLAT CIRCLE

EXAMINING *TRUE DETECTIVE*, SEASON ONE

TIME IS A FLAT CIRCLE

EXAMINING *TRUE DETECTIVE*, SEASON ONE

MELISSA MILAZZO

with Adam and Mark Stewart

SEQUART ORGANIZATION   EDWARDSVILLE, ILLINOIS

Time is a Flat Circle: Examining *True Detective*, Season One
by Melissa Milazzo, with Adam and Mark Stewart

First edition, January 2019, ISBN 978-1-9405-8920-6.

Cover by Kevin Colden. Book design by Julian Darius. Interior art is © HBO.

Published by Sequart Organization. Edited by Mike Phillips. Assistant edited by Tim Bavlnka, Parker Bray, Keith Howell, and Karra Shimabukuro.

For more information about other titles in this series, visit Sequart.org/books.

Dedication

For Tone Milazzo, the Michael Jordan of being a husband.

Contents

Introduction

The first season of *True Detective* is the same old story. It's a buddy cop show with a pair of mismatched detectives who play by their own rules. It's hard-boiled sleuths in dive bars and shootouts, trading dialogue sharper than a knife to the back. It's a black-as-night noir with corruption and existential dread lurking around every corner. It's a Southern gothic draped in rotting vines and unspeakable family secrets. It's cosmic horror where the thin veil of reality is slipping and visions of an uncaring universe drive men to madness. *True Detective* is an amalgamation of pulp genres that have been done to death, and yet, there is a strangeness lurking in all the familiarity.

True Detective[1] premiered on HBO on January 12, 2014 and it was an immediate hit, becoming the most watched freshman show in the network's history at that time.[2] Nic Pizzolatto's writing, along with director Cary Joji Fukunaga's vision, T Bone Burnett's musical contributions, and the brilliant performances by leads Matthew McConaughey and Woody Harrelson proved a winning combination. As each new episode aired, it spawned hundreds of

---

[1] Note that for the sake of brevity any mention of *True Detective* in this volume refers to the *first* season of *True Detective* and *only* the first season. The second and third seasons of the show feature separate stories and different casts and are not covered in this book.

[2] Andreeva, Nellie. "'True Detective' Now Most Watched HBO Freshman Series Ever." Deadline. April 15, 2014. Accessed September 15, 2018. https://deadline.com/2014/04/true-detective-now-most-watched-hbo-freshman-series-ever-715055/.

articles, blogs, and podcasts, each vying to untangle the show's non-linear narrative and dense web of literary and philosophical allusions. The lush, haunting visuals of the show inspired a blossom of fan art, while the eminently quotable dialogue was transformed into memes and parody.

Some critics hailed the show as revolutionary, dubbing the single writer/ single director format as auteur storytelling brought to the small screen. From its conception, the story was intended to run for a single season and have a concrete beginning and end. Additionally, Pizzolatto and Fukunaga retained tight control over creative decisions, achieving a clarity of vision not often possible when each episode of a show is the result of a different writer and director. As critic Andrew Romano notes, "not every story is best told by committee or as an open-ended epic."[3] Part of the appeal of *True Detective* is that each scene is branded with the show's distinctive look, feel, and sound, achieving a singular mood to match the journey of its memorable characters.

Although critical response to the first season was largely positive, there were notable dissenting opinions. *The New Yorker*'s Emily Nussbaum found the show to be pretentious pulp, citing the flat female characters and "disposable female bodies."[4] The show generated think pieces debating whether the show was misogynist or if it merely portrayed misogyny.[5] Meanwhile, in a completely different corner of the internet, fans within the weird fiction community took issue with the praise Nic Pizzolatto received for the originality of his script, noting that Pizzolatto used the work of Robert W. Chambers (*The King in Yellow*) as the basis for the show's occult lore. They also took issue with the extent to which Rust Cohle's haunting dialogue was influenced by the

---

[3] Romano, Andrew. "'True Detective' Review: You Have to Watch HBO's Revolutionary Crime Classic." The Daily Beast. January 11, 2014. Accessed September 15, 2018. https://www.thedailybeast.com/true-detective-review-you-have-to-watch-hbos-revolutionary-crime-classic.
[4] Nussbaum, Emily. "Cool Story, Bro." *The New Yorker*. June 19, 2017. Accessed September 15, 2018. https://www.newyorker.com/magazine/2014/03/03/cool-story-bro.
[5] Hurley, Kameron. "Some Men Are More Monstrous Than Others: On True Detective's Men & Monsters." Kameron Hurley. April 16, 2014. Accessed September 15, 2018. https://www.kameronhurley.com/some-men-are-more-monstrous-than-others-on-true-detectives-men-monsters/.

philosophical writings of Thomas Ligotti (*The Conspiracy Against Mankind*).[6]

What was lost in all the controversy, hype, and fan theories about *True Detective* was a more in-depth look at what the show achieves as a genre work. At its core, *True Detective* is a cross-genre narrative, blending elements of hardboiled detective, noir, Southern gothic, and cosmic horror. Cross-genre work is not new, nor is it new to television,[7] but in the first season of *True Detective* Nic Pizzolatto's cross-genre storytelling reinvigorates a familiar story about cops chasing a killer, turning it into an opportunity to examine the nature of self, society, faith, and even reality.

This volume examines the first season of *True Detective* through the lens of genre to identify how Pizzolatto and Fukunaga's use of multiple genres defines and amplifies a set of themes within the narrative. The focus here is less on the distinctions between genres and more on the places where they overlap. These points of intersection form the thematic pillars of *True Detective*: corruption of the self, corruption of society, the malleable nature of reality, and the meaning (or lack thereof) of life.

In the following essays, I apply close textual analysis to all eight episodes of the first season. This approach includes literary aspects of the show such as plot, dialogue, character, and symbolism, as well as directorial elements like editing and cinematography. In the spirit of staying close to the text, I use lines of dialogue as pull quotes throughout the essays. That, and because the dialogue is just too fun to be used without a little humor.

Each of the following chapters focus on single genre and how elements of the genre forward the key themes of *True Detective*. Both the first and the last chapters take a more foundational approach, looking at elements that inform the genres at work in *True Detective*. The first chapter looks to the roots of genre, building on the idea of the Cretan labyrinth myth as the precursor of detective fiction and interpreting *True Detective* as a retelling of that ancient tale about a man, a monster, and a labyrinth. The final chapter focuses on the

---

[6] Steele, Justin. "*True Detective*'s Nic Pizzolatto on Ligotti." The Arkham Digest. January 01, 1970. Accessed September 15, 2018.
http://www.arkhamdigest.com/2014/01/true-detectives-nic-pizzolatto-on.html.
[7] British television drama *The Prisoner* (1967) combined elements of the spy thriller genre with science fiction, allegory, and psychological horror. More recent examples of cross-genre works on television include HBO's *True Blood* (paranormal romance) and *Westworld* (science-fiction western).

anti-natalist philosophy that defines much of Cohle's character, as well as the moral underpinnings of the comic horror genre.

The appendices in this volume provide a home for materials that highlight the wide array of media that influenced *True Detective*. Primary among these is a contribution by Adam Stewart and Mark Stewart. Their "Guide to *True Detective* and Weird Comic Book Fiction," explores the many comic book tributaries that flow into *True Detective*. Adam and Mark's work is a great introduction to how comic books can inspire television and film outside the superhero genre.

Music plays an integral part in setting the mood of *True Detective*, so any discussion of the show would feel incomplete without it. "In the Groove" focuses on the musical direction provided by the legendary T Bone Burnett. This appendix details every song appearing in show, along with notes about the song's history and significance to the scene in which it appeared. "This Kind of Thing Doesn't Happen in a Vacuum" covers the Louisiana true crime case that inspired the allegations against the Tuttle ministries in *True Detective*. "Just the Facts, Ma'am" chronicles the controversy sparked by weird fiction fans, a blog, and accusations of plagiarism. The final appendix is a recommended reading and viewing list. Compiled with the help of Miguel Rodriguez, founder of the *Horrible Imaginings* film festival and podcast,[8] this list should help fans of *True Detective* find new stories to scratch that same itch.

Now that the vision has been articulated, it's time to cue the music, pour a drink, and mainline the secret truths of the *True Detective* universe.

---

[8] hifilmfest.com.

ESSAYS:

That's the Genre, Not the Title

There's a Monster at the End: The Labyrinth in *True Detective*

In the first episode of *True Detective*, Marty Hart lists the types of detective he's seen over the course of his career. "The bully, the charmer... the brain. Any of those types could be a good detective and any of those types could be an incompetent shitheel."[1] As Hart notes, a detective isn't defined by his personality; he is defined by his work as an investigator. Although many types of detective appear in the various genres of detective fiction, their investigations tend to follow a pattern. Should the story feature a classical detective like Sherlock Holmes or a hard-boiled shamus like Sam Spade, the initial investigation quickly expands into a much larger mystery, a case that leads the detective through a winding maze of possibilities and dead-ends. This shared pattern exists because all varieties of the detective genre, including *True Detective*, have a shared ancestor in the myth of the labyrinth.

The myth begins with King Minos of Crete ordering the architect Daedalus to build a labyrinth to contain the Minotaur, a monster born with the head of a bull and the body of a man. After imprisoning the Minotaur, King Minos fed the monster with human sacrifices kidnapped from nearby Athens. Theseus, prince

---

[1] *True Detective*. "The Long Bright Dark." Episode 1. Directed by Cary Joji Fukunaga. Written by Nic Pizzolatto. HBO. January 12, 2014.

of Athens, was understandably upset by this turn of events and set out for Crete to find the labyrinth and slay the Minotaur. Along the way, he met and fell in love with Ariadne, who aided Theseus by giving him a sword and a clue (ball or skein) of thread. This foresight was the key to Theseus's success, for the thread was all he had to lead him safely out of the labyrinth after he killed the Minotaur. The myth ends with a triumphant Theseus escaping Crete with Ariadne at his side.

At first glance, the myth of the labyrinth reads as more of a heroic tale than a mystery, but "while they aren't always obvious, the influences of the myth of the maze are certainly evident"[2] in the detective genre. When imagined through the lens of the detective genre, the Minotaur becomes the criminal, trapped in the harsh concrete labyrinth of streets and skyscrapers. The ball of thread becomes a trail of clues to be followed by the detective, who serves as the modern-day Theseus.

> This sort of thing doesn't happen in a vacuum.
> — Rust Cohle

The significance of the labyrinth in hard-boiled detective fiction and film noir is a well-established theme for many academics. Starting with Foster Hirsch's analysis in *The Dark Side of the Screen*, a succession of writers have established that the labyrinth in hard-boiled noir is more than the dangerous city streets the detective prowls each night. It is also the mapping of corrupt cops, crooked politicians, and how power really flows through the city. At its deepest level, the labyrinth is a cypher for the inner workings of the detective, a psychological space where he must confront uncomfortable truths about himself and about the human condition. The interior of the labyrinth is where hard-boiled noir detectives like Marty Hart and Rust Cohle must navigate their way through what is known and what is yet to be discovered, what is truth and what is illusion, what is right and what is wrong.

---

[2] Abrams, Jerold J. "From Sherlock Holmes to the Hard-Boiled Detective in Film Noir." *The Philosophy of Film Noir*, edited by Mark T. Conard. Lexington: University Press of Kentucky, 2007.

In *Semiotics and the Philosophy of Language*, Umberto Eco identifies three types of labyrinth (or maze): the classical, the mannerist, and the rhizomatic.[3] The "classical Greek maze" is the version with Theseus, the Minotaur, Ariadne, and her string. According to Eco, it is possible to escape a "classical" maze. Escaping the classical maze is not easy (hence the need for Ariadne's string), but it is also not the greatest hurdle to a hero's success. In this version of the maze, the greatest threat comes from the Minotaur. Eco defines the "mannerist maze" as the next development of the form. It focuses on distorted perception. Much like an M.C. Escher lithograph, the pathways in the "mannerist maze" follow impossible geometries and defy logical explanation. These physical distortions are symbolic of rapid changes to society. Eco explains that in the "mannerist maze" there is no need for a Minotaur, as "social fragmentation, moral skepticism, cultural pluralism" pose greater threats to the hero than any monster.

The final version Eco identifies is the "rhizomatic maze." A rhizome is a term used both in philosophy and botany, though the botanical model offers a better visual for the concept. Rhizomes are the horizontal stems of some plants which send out roots and shoots in all directions. Ferns, grasses, hops, and seaweed are all rhizomatic plants whereas a tree, which grows vertically, is non-rhizomatic. When philosophers imagined a rhizome shaped labyrinth they found that it, "has no center; it has no perimeter; and, worst of all, it has no way out."[4] Thus, the rhizomatic maze is a labyrinth of endless paths and endless clues but no escape. Like the mannerist maze, there is no Minotaur in the rhizomatic maze. The threat comes from the disordered and inescapable shape of the labyrinth. When escape is impossible, the maze becomes the monster.

Building on Eco's work, critic Jerold J. Abrams posits that the labyrinth as it appears in film noir is the rhizomatic type. He provides analysis of several noir classics, noting that the mazes which appear in these films are often self-perpetuating and inescapable. A notable example comes from *The Third Man* (Carol Reed, 1949). The climactic scenes of this film take place in a labyrinthine underground sewer, a setting symbolic of both the criminal underworld and the

---

[3] Eco, Umberto. *Semiotics and the Philosophy of Language*. Bloomington: Indiana University Press, 1986.

[4] Abrams, Jerold J. "From Sherlock Holmes to the Hard-Boiled Detective in Film Noir." *The Philosophy of Film Noir*, edited by Mark T. Conard. Lexington: University Press of Kentucky, 2007.

impossible maze of clues and questions trapping a detective. At the end of the film, one of the main characters nearly escapes the labyrinth of the sewer and the criminals chasing him, but dies just as his hand breaches the sewer grate. For Abrams, this scene summarizes the plight of a detective trapped in a rhizomatic maze. Not only did the character fail to escape the physical labyrinth of the sewer; he also remained trapped within the wider, rhizomatic labyrinth of the criminal underworld. "There was no escape either way."[5]

True Detective, like every other genre story before it, does not take place in a vacuum. Therefore, analyzing the type of labyrinth present in *True Detective* can provide an Ariadne's string of clues to help the viewer interpret the story and its ending. *True Detective* exhibits elements of the classical labyrinth and the classical detective story. At the same time, there are strong hard-boiled and film noir elements, hinting that the labyrinth in the narrative should be an inescapable, rhizomatic type. There is an inherent tension between these two types of labyrinth – one that can be escaped and one that cannot – that propels the narrative of *True Detective*, and that sparked much of the debate around whether the first season's finale was a satisfactory ending to the story or an inappropriately happy ending.

> You, these people, this place. It's like you eat your fucking young…
> — Rust Cohle

An argument for a classical labyrinth in *True Detective* can be founded on the parallels between characters in *True Detective* and the myth of the Cretan labyrinth, particularly the roles of Theseus, Ariadne, and the Minotaur.

The detective in the Cretan myth is Theseus, the Athenian who travels to a strange land to stop the youth of his city from being abducted and ritually sacrificed. Rust Cohle clearly fills this role in *True Detective*. As a Texan, Cohle is an outsider to Vermilion Parish, Louisiana where the narrative is set. Cohle struggles in his new environment, unable to understand Marty Hart's acceptance of a status quo where religious and political authority is consolidated in the Tuttle family. Although Cohle does not come to Vermilion Parish with the express goal of stopping the Yellow King cult sacrifices, he does come to Louisiana with a sense of purpose. Detectives Gilbough and Papina ask Cohle why he didn't just retire and collect disability after being injured while

---

[5] Ibid.

working undercover. Cohle replies, "the body is not one member, but many. Now are they many, but of one body."[6] Cohle's answer points to his desire to rejoin society and contribute to the welfare of his community. Having specific goals make Theseus and Cohle proactive characters, seeking out new information, chasing leads, and initiating contact with possible witnesses. Cohle fits the mold of the classical detective, as he, like Theseus, is intent on solving a mystery and ready to run headlong into the labyrinth in pursuit of a monster.

Although Theseus is remembered as the hero of the Cretan myth, his success is not possible without his partner Ariadne. The daughter of King Minos, Ariadne is part of the existing power structure in Crete. She uses her position to provide Theseus with information about the labyrinth — namely that escaping it will be one of the most challenging parts of the ordeal. In *True Detective*, Marty Hart fills the Ariadne role. As a veteran of the police force and a Louisiana native, Hart understands the complex tangle of politics, family ties, and departmental corruption and uses this knowledge to help Cohle navigate his way through the Yellow King cult investigation. In the 2012 phase of the investigation, Hart's connections prove particularly useful, as his private investigator credentials give Hart and Cohle access to the tax records that allow them to make the connection between a little girl's report of a "spaghetti monster with green ears"[7] and Errol Childress's current location.

For all the jokes about "bromance" in popular commentary on *True Detective*, there is a romantic element to Hart's relationship with Cohle. Just as Ariadne fell in love with the foreign Theseus, Hart is fascinated by Cohle and the novelty he represents. The romance between the detectives is not a result of sexual desire,[8] but the result of the mystery and excitement Cohle brings to Hart's otherwise stagnant life. At the outset of the narrative, Hart attempts to distract himself from his failing marriage, the responsibilities of fatherhood, and the grim realities of aging by chasing younger women. These activities do not provide him with the stimulation and affirmation he seeks. Instead this comes

---

[6] *True Detective*. "Seeing Things." Episode 2. Directed by Cary Joji Fukunaga. Written by Nic Pizzolatto. HBO. January 19, 2014. Note that Cohle's line paraphrases 1 Corinthians 14, "For the body does not consist of one part, but many."
[7] *True Detective*. "The Long Bright Dark." Episode 1. Directed by Cary Joji Fukunaga. Written by Nic Pizzolatto. HBO. January 12, 2014.
[8] Although Hart and Cohle's relationship is ripe for analysis through the lens of Queer theory.

from Cohle, who bothers Hart on a visceral level. Cohle challenges Hart's world view by introducing him to philosophy and calling him out on the hypocrisy of espousing family values while cheating on his wife. Hart may complain about having a combative partner who says, "odd shit like [he] can smell a psycho's fear or [he's] in someone's faded memory of a town,"[9] but Cohle's weirdness invites Hart to step outside his ordinary life in a way he has never been able to do before.

" HOLMES GAVE ME A SKETCH OF THE EVENTS."

Sherlock Holmes and Doctor Watson. Illustration by Sidney Paget. Published in "The Adventure of Silver Blaze," which appeared in *The Strand Magazine* in December 1892.

---

[9] *True Detective*. "The Long Bright Dark." Episode 1. Directed by Cary Joji Fukunaga. Written by Nic Pizzolatto. HBO. January 12, 2014.

The key dynamic between Cohle and Hart in their respective Theseus / Ariadne roles is that Cohle is proactive and self-determining, whereas Hart is reactive and supportive. After their falling out and Cohle's subsequent resignation from the police force, Hart drops the Yellow King cult investigation professionally and personally. Hart only returns to the case in 2012 because Cohle finds him and badgers him into action. A similar active Theseus / reactive Ariadne dynamic exists in many classic detective tales, notably in Sir Arthur Conan Doyle's Holmes and Watson. Sherlock Holmes, in the Theseus role famously cries, "Come, Watson, come... The game's afoot!"[10] and Doctor Watson, performing the reactive Ariadne role, follows the call to adventure.

Another argument for the classical labyrinth in *True Detective* is the existence of a literal monster in the labyrinth of the investigation in the form of Errol Childress. Like the Minotaur from the Cretan labyrinth, Errol Childress is the unwanted child of a powerful family and his deformity is linked to sins of his father.

In the Cretan myth, King Minos is the father of the Minotaur. When he ascended to the throne, King Minos was obligated to sacrifice a beautiful white bull to show honor to the gods. Overcome with greed, King Minos ignored his duty and kept the bull for himself. The gods had their revenge on the selfish king. They made his wife fall in love with the great white bull. She lusted after the animal, copulated with it and birthed a deformed child with the head of bull and the body of a man. Thus, the birth of the Minotaur is a direct result of King Minos's greed and hubris. Similarly, Errol Childress is the illegitimate grandchild of Sam Tuttle, patriarch of the influential Tuttle family. The Tuttle family's occult worship of The Yellow King also mirrors the religious perversion of King Minos in the Cretan myth. Like the Minotaur, Errol Childress is the result of his family's greed and lust.

The parallels continue with the half-man, half-beast nature of the Minotaur and the bestial imagery associated with Errol Childress in *True Detective*. Instead of having the head of a bull like the Minotaur, the lower half of Childress's face is covered with burns (inflicted upon him by his father). Combined with his massive size and deep, bellowing voice, the waxy scars on Childress's face give him a frightening, animalistic air. Childress's association

---

[10] Doyle, Arthur Conan. "The Return of Sherlock Holmes." *The New Annotated Sherlock Holmes*. Edited by Leslie S. Klinger. New York: W.W. Norton, 2005.

with antlers – placing them on the heads of his victims and using them to adorn the alter of his shrine to the Yellow King – also evokes the horns atop the Minotaur's bullish head. In a very subtle reference (or perhaps just a happy accident), the idea of a bull is also present in the labyrinthine architecture of Carcosa. The domed ceiling of the room where Childress built his altar to the Yellow King features a small, round window – an oculus, from the Latin for "eye." In French, this type of window is known as *œil de boeuf*, or "bull's eye."

In both the Cretan myth and *True Detective*, the physical edifice of the labyrinth is linked with a powerful patriarchal figure and his desire to hide his deformed offspring. Note that Errol Childress shares his dilapidated home with a female relative (sister or cousin), who is intellectually disabled and likely is also being hidden from public view by the respectable branch of the Tuttle family. These powerful men hide their unwanted offspring out of shame and a futile desire to contain the repercussions of their own greed and hubris. The Minotaur is proof that the gods cursed King Minos for greed and failure to make a proper sacrifice. For the Tuttle family, murderous Errol is proof that the Tuttle dynasty is not a wholesome group devoted to Christian values. Although the Minotaur and Childress are both isolated from society (albeit to a much lesser degree in Childress's case), their monstrous desires cannot be contained. In an ironic twist, King Minos and the heads of the Tuttle family must make sacrifices to appease their misbegotten offspring as a punishment for failing to practice the traditional religions of their community.

In the Cretan myth, every seven years the Minotaur receives seven youths and seven maidens from the city of Athens. These unfortunate souls are either eaten by the Minotaur or die of exhaustion while searching for escape from the labyrinth. Similarly, Errol Childress murders children and young women in the labyrinthine tunnels behind his plantation house. When Detectives Hart and Cohle finally confront Childress in his labyrinth, they find evidence of previous sacrifices: a human skeleton wrapped in a shroud and crowned with antlers, a moldering pile of children's clothing, and a macabre altar constructed of skulls, sticks, and a tattered yellow robe. Childress's Carcosa is a slaughter house, an updated version of the Minotaur's labyrinth. Both structures are shrines to the death of innocents and the endurance of systemic evil. Sacrifices enter, but only the monsters survive.

The similarities between Errol Childress and the Minotaur make one of the strongest arguments for *True Detective* being a classical labyrinth. The existence of a physical monster means it is possible for the detectives to slay the monster and successfully escape the labyrinth.

> Everything we've ever done or will do, we're going to do over and over again…
> — Rust Cohle

While there are similarities between characters in *True Detective* and the classic labyrinth myth, there is some evidence of a film noir, or rhizomatic labyrinth in *True Detective*. Much of the case for a rhizomatic labyrinth comes from Rust Cohle's philosophy and fatalism.

Cohle identifies himself as a pessimist in the first episode of the show. He holds a bleak worldview wherein all life is suffering and the only hope for escape is to embrace death, "stop reproducing, walk hand in hand into extinction, one last midnight - brothers and sisters opting out of a raw deal."[11] Arguing the futility of existence isn't a trait associated with heroic characters or the classical detective. It is, however, in line with the jaded worldview of a film noir private eye. The noir detective sees the seedy underbelly of his city and knows that most of the high society folks are as debauched and puerile as the lowliest gutter dweller – or as Cohle puts it, "it's all one ghetto, man, a giant gutter in outer space."[12] Cohle's idea that the whole universe is corrupted falls perfectly in line with the concept of a rhizomatic maze. It reinforces the idea that no matter how hard Hart and Cohle work to solve their cases or how far away from Vermilion Parish they run, they will still find themselves trapped in a "world where nothing is solved."[13]

The noir detective is more isolated than his classical counterpart, in part because of his cynical worldview and in part because he is unapologetic about the social friction his philosophy causes. Humphrey Bogart voices this sentiment with pitch-perfect sarcasm when playing the role of Philip Marlowe in the film noir classic, *The Big Sleep*. "I don't mind if you don't like my manners." He

---

[11] *True Detective*. "The Long Bright Dark." Episode 1. Directed by Cary Joji Fukunaga. Written by Nic Pizzolatto. HBO. January 12, 2014. Note that this line of Cohle's dialogue is heavily influenced by the anti-natalist philosophy in Thomas Ligotti's work.
[12] Ibid.
[13] *True Detective*. "The Secret Fate of All Life." Episode 5. Directed by Cary Joji Fukunaga. Written by Nic Pizzolatto. HBO. February 16, 2014.

sneers, "they're pretty bad. I grieve over them during the long winter evenings."[14] This sort of behavior prevents the noir detective from connecting with a faithful Ariadne character who could provide him help in escaping the maze. Cohle often exhibits a noir detective's world-weary arrogance when interacting with Marty Hart. Early in their partnership, Hart asks Cohle to stop "saying odd shit," because it's unprofessional. Cohle responds with, "seeing as how long it's taken me to reconcile my nature, I can't figure I'd forgo it on your account, Marty."[15] Part of the noir detective's refusal of help from possible Ariadne characters stems from understanding the rhizomatic nature of the labyrinth in which he is trapped. Trusting other characters or accepting help from them will only complicate the detective's job, prompting more questions, more clues, more possible paths that must be investigated. For the noir detective, staying true to his principles and avoiding entanglements is the simplest way to navigate the complex labyrinth of an investigation.

The inescapable nature of the rhizomatic labyrinth of film noir has ties to the nihilist philosophy which permeates the genre, specifically to Friedrich Nietzsche's idea of the eternal recurrence. Nietzsche proposed the eternal recurrence as a thought experiment, asking his reader to imagine life as an eternal loop with no beginning or end... "and there will be nothing new in it, but every pain and every joy and every thought and sigh... will have to return to you, all in the same succession and sequence."[16]

As they investigate the Yellow King case, Detectives Hart and Cohle enter a version of Nietzsche's unending cycle. They enter the labyrinthine investigation in 1995 with the murder of Dora Lange, then spend over a decade chasing the same leads and hitting a dead end each time their investigation leads to the Tuttle family. In the latter half of the narrative, Hart and Cohle try get a fresh perspective on the case, but they inevitably return to the same locations, digging up the same names and the same clues. Several characters from the first investigation return in the later portion of the story. Reverend Tuttle, revival preacher Joel Theriot, detective Steve Geraci, and Beth, the underage

---

[14] *The Big Sleep*. Directed by Howard Hawks. 1946.

[15] *True Detective*. "The Long Bright Dark." Episode 1. Directed by Cary Joji Fukunaga. Written by Nic Pizzolatto. HBO. January 12, 2014.

[16] Nietzsche, Friedrich. *The Gay Science: With a Prelude in Rhymes and an Appendix of Songs*. Translated by Walter Kaufmann. NY, NY: Vintage Books, 1974. Aphorism 341, "The Greatest Weight"

prostitute from the trailer park brothel, all appear in the original 1995 investigative cycle and again in the later cycle, evoking a sense of *déjà vu*.

Humphrey Bogart gets metafictional as detective Philip Marlowe in a screenshot from the trailer for *The Big Sleep* (Howard Hawks, 1946). Bogart is reading a copy of the 1939 Raymond Chandler novel which inspired the film.

While trapped in the rhizomatic labyrinth of the Yellow King investigation, Detectives Cohle and Hart are also trapped in their respective Theseus and Ariadne roles. The closing scenes of episode six, "Haunted Houses," are set in 2012. Hart is still in the passive Ariadne role, being chased off the road by Cohle, who is still playing the aggressive Theseus role. After a tense reunion, the former partners agree to have a beer and talk, but director Cary Joji Fukunaga dispels any hope that the men have grown or changed over the decade they spent apart. He does so with a single image – the broken taillight on Cohle's pickup truck. The same taillight that Hart and Cohle broke during the fistfight that marked the end of their partnership. It is an unhealed scar and a reminder that although time has passed, nothing has changed between the detectives.

After spending decades trapped in the labyrinth of the Yellow King investigation, a grizzled Cohle clearly sees the walls of the rhizomatic labyrinth around him. In the 2012 interview with Detectives Gilbough and Papina, Cohle paraphrases Nietzsche's unending cycle. Cohle asks the younger men to imagine that, "all your life, all your love, all your hate, all your memories, all your pain ...it was all the same dream, a dream that you had inside a locked room."[17]

Marty Hart and Rust Cohle are unable to escape the labyrinthine investigation of the Yellow King cult. *True Detective*, season 1, episode 7, "After You've Gone." HBO.

> Someone once told me time is a flat circle.
> — Rust Cohle

Cohle's talk of unending cycles ties into one of the main motifs in *True Detective*: the spiral. It appears as the sigil of the Yellow King cult and manifests in Cohle's hallucinations as a flock of birds curling in formation above an abandoned church. The spiral motif extends to the natural world as well in the form of hurricanes. Though their massive, whirling arms do not appear on screen, hurricanes Rita, Andrew, and Katrina are all mentioned by name in *True Detective*. The physical power of these spiral storms drives residents of the Gulf Coast into an unending cycle of destruction, loss, and rebuilding. However, the most significant spiral is the one Hart and Cohle find painted on Dora Lange's

---

[17] *True Detective*. "The Secret Fate of All Life." Episode 5. Directed by Cary Joji Fukunaga. Written by Nic Pizzolatto. HBO. February 16, 2014.

body. This spiral is where the detectives enter the labyrinth of the Yellow King cult investigation.

Like much of the other evidence in *True Detective,* the spiral does not offer a clear answer to what type of labyrinth exists in the narrative. The spiral can be read as corresponding to themes of a noir rhizomatic labyrinth, as a spiral is a line that circles itself, winding and growing but always retaining the same shape. The repetition of a spiral evokes a sense of inevitability; once the pattern is established, it will never change. These aspects of a spiral correspond with Nietzsche's eternal recurrence and the idea of a detective being trapped within a world of crime. However, the spiral can also be read as a classical labyrinth. The open end of a spiral forms an entrance, an invitation to follow the curved path of empty space between the lines. It also forms an exit, making the spiral a labyrinth with a means of escape – a feature unique to the classical labyrinth. Additionally, depictions of the Cretan labyrinth usually interpret it as a spiral with a single, non-branching path that leads to a central chamber where the Minotaur dwells.

Redrawn version of a carved Renaissance gem depicting the Minotaur at the center of a labyrinth. Note that the Minotaur is represented here as a man's head and torso joined to a bull's body, in reverse of the Classical tradition showing a bull's head on a man's body. MAFFEI, P. A. "Gemmae Antiche," 1709, Pt. IV, pl. 31.

Whether it's read as a classical labyrinth or a noir rhizomatic labyrinth, the spiral in *True Detective* does not support branching possibilities. Instead, it evokes the idea that there is a single, inevitable conclusion, a truth which can be found if one follows the track of the labyrinth all the way to the end. As the detectives prepare for their confrontation with Errol Childress, Rust Cohle reveals that he is looking to escape the labyrinth of the Yellow King cult investigation by any means necessary. "My life has been a circle of violence and degradation for as I can remember." He tells Hart, "I'm looking to tie it off."[18] In a noir rhizomatic labyrinth, death is the only option for escape and Cohle's comment reveals his assumption that death is his only remaining option to end the eternal recurrence in which he is trapped.

> I'm not supposed to be here.
> — Rust Cohle

By the rules of a noir rhizomatic labyrinth, Cohle should die in Carcosa, in a futile gesture of self-sacrifice that ultimately fixes nothing about the world. Instead, Pizzolatto plays by the rules of the classical labyrinth, having Cohle escape with the help of Hart. Fulfilling his Ariadne role, Hart gives Cohle the support he needs to successfully escape the labyrinth. He distracts Errol Childress long enough for Cohle to recover his gun and kill Childress, as well as doing what he can to help the wounded Cohle stay alive until help arrives. When Cohle wakes up in the hospital, he has physically escaped, but his mind is clearly still within the labyrinth, as he complains to Hart that they didn't "get" the whole Yellow King cult. Hart smiles, shakes his head, and reminds Cohle, "that ain't what kind of world this is... but we got ours."[19] Hart's perspective is exactly the lifeline Cohle needs to keep himself from re-entering the labyrinth after he has just barely escaped it with his life. Without Hart, Cohle would be doomed to keep repeating the same pattern of self-destructive behaviors until he met a bloody and futile end.

---

[18] *True Detective*. "After You've Gone." Episode 7. Directed by Cary Joji Fukunaga. Written by Nic Pizzolatto. HBO. March 2, 2014.
[19] *True Detective*. "Form and Void." Episode 8. Directed by Cary Joji Fukunaga. Written by Nic Pizzolatto. HBO. March 9, 2014.

Hart's reminder about what kind of world the detectives inhabit is a callback to Cohle's view that "this is a world where nothing is solved,"[20] but Hart doesn't fully accept the idea of being trapped in a noir rhizomatic labyrinth. By adding "... but we got ours,"[21] Hart validates Cohle as having achieved his objective. Like Theseus, Cohle slayed the monster in the labyrinth and lived to tell the tale. Theseus was not tasked with punishing all the corrupt officials of Crete that made the labyrinth possible, as such wide scale retribution is well outside the scope of any detective tale. Similarly, Cohle does not need to hold himself responsible for fixing all the corruption in the state of Louisiana. Indeed, the powers one man would need to achieve such a feat would render Cohle a superhero rather than a detective. Hart's line reminding Cohle of both his success and his limitations supports the classical labyrinth reading of *True Detective*. Hart and Cohle are only responsible for slaying *their* monster and if they succeed, they have earned their escape.

An ending where the private eye walks away from the labyrinth isn't unheard of in noir. In fact, Hart's line echoes Roman Polanski's 1974 neo-noir, *Chinatown*. The final scene of the film features Private Investigator Jake Gittes (Jack Nicholson) staring at the body of a murdered woman, knowing all his detective work and the truths he uncovered did nothing to save her. Jake Gittes allows himself to be led away by his associate who utters the famous line. "Forget it Jake. It's Chinatown."[22] Polanski's ending, while technically allowing Gittes to walk away from the labyrinth investigation, is still in keeping with the noir idea of the world as fundamentally flawed and unfixable. Pizzolatto's ending in *True Detective* keeps the pessimistic view of the world, but offers an optimistic view of Hart and Cohle's ability to effect change in themselves.

> If we were getting engaged I would have got a nicer ribbon.
> — Marty Hart

In the final episode, "Form and Void," the scene between Cohle and Hart outside of the hospital stands out from the rest of the season, because it is the

---

[20] *True Detective*. "The Secret Fate of All Life." Episode 5. Directed by Cary Joji Fukunaga. Written by Nic Pizzolatto. HBO. February 16, 2014.

[21] *True Detective*. "Form and Void." Episode 8. Directed by Cary Joji Fukunaga. Written by Nic Pizzolatto. HBO. March 9, 2014.

[22] *Chinatown*. Directed by Roman Polanski. Hollywood, CA.: Paramount Home Video, 1974. DVD.

first interaction between the characters outside of the labyrinth. Just as the labyrinth forced the detectives into repetitive cycles of investigation, it also kept them trapped in their roles – Cohle as Theseus, the driven investigator and Hart as Ariadne, the faithful helper. It's only when they are free from the confines of the investigation that the detectives can experience any kind of change or growth.

The change in Hart's character comes through when he gives Cohle a key to his apartment. Hart does not *ask* Cohle to live with him; he *tells* Cohle that they'll be living together. The shift is subtle, but it marks the first time Hart actively defines the terms of his relationship with Cohle. From his plea that Cohle make the car, "a place of silent reflection from now on,"[23] in the first episode to his ineffectual warning to stay away from Maggie, Hart's attempts to set boundaries while he was in the labyrinth were always reactionary. Outside the labyrinth, Hart has the freedom to be proactive and change the dynamic of his relationship with Cohle. Hart's joke about getting a "nicer ribbon"[24] serves as a subtle reminder of the ties the two men share and the thread of clues that made their escape from the labyrinth possible.

The change in Cohle's character is more dramatic, as he was deeply lost within the labyrinth of the investigation and thus more trapped in his Theseus role. While inside the labyrinth, Cohle embodied a relentless drive for answers. His monomania left him trapped in an endless recurrence where "...nothing can grow. Nothing can become. Nothing changes."[25] He entered the labyrinth of the Yellow King cult investigation as a brittle man, clinging to sanity and clearly not having processed the tragic death of his daughter. Inside the labyrinth, Cohle could not address his personal issues; there was a monster loose in Vermilion Parish and he was responsible for stopping it. Having escaped the labyrinth, Cohle has no string of clues to follow, no ferocious Minotaur to confront. For the first time in decades, he is free to grow, to become, to change. It is only once he escapes that Cohle can look up and imagine a different story for himself.

[23] *True Detective*. "The Long Bright Dark." Episode 1. Directed by Cary Joji Fukunaga. Written by Nic Pizzolatto. HBO. January 12, 2014.

[24] *True Detective*. "Form and Void." Episode 8. Directed by Cary Joji Fukunaga. Written by Nic Pizzolatto. HBO. March 9, 2014.

[25] *True Detective*. "The Secret Fate of All Life." Episode 5. Directed by Cary Joji Fukunaga. Written by Nic Pizzolatto. HBO. February 16, 2014.

It's just one story, the oldest.
— Rust Cohle

Pizzolatto's use of both the noir rhizomatic labyrinth and the classical labyrinth in *True Detective* created a unique tension in the narrative, but ultimately proved disappointing for some fans. Many viewers hoped for a more noir ending – one with more death and futility – but the "happy" ending did not come out of left field. Pizzolatto laid the groundwork for a classical maze throughout narrative and hinted that the escape from the labyrinth was possible with the spiral motif. Pizzolatto's real success in *True Detective* is in creating a story that sparks debate. It breathes new life into an ancient and oft-told story about a man, a monster, a maze, and a trail of clues.

You're Creating a Maze for Yourself: The Noir Labyrinth of Identity

For hardboiled and film noir detectives, crime is not a disease; it is a symptom of human society.[1] The fact that crime is an inescapable outgrowth of human needs and societal pressures is the foundation of a noir detective's world. As a result, the detective's investigation of a crime is intrinsically linked to an exploration of human motivations. Just as the detective must question the motivation of suspects and victims, he must also question the motivations behind his own behavior. Operating alone in a tough world, he cannot afford to lie to himself if he wants to solve the case and stay alive.

In *True Detective*, Rust Cohle's struggles with his motivation and identity culminate in episode four, "Who Goes There," in the six-minute tracking shot following Cohle's run through the Hoston projects. The shot is a fresh take on the noir convention of using the tall buildings and back alleys of a big city to evoke the walls of a labyrinth. Rather than relying on the standard urban architecture, director Cary Joji Fukunaga creates the same sense of

---

[1] Chandler, Raymond. The Long Goodbye. Stellar Books, 2013. "Crime isn't a disease. It's a symptom. We're a big rough rich wild people and crime is the price we pay for it... crime is just the dirty side of the sharp dollar."

claustrophobia and menace by using a sprawling public housing division filled with single-story buildings and wide expanses of lawn. The failed stash house raid and subsequent chase through the projects presents the noir world in miniature: a detective playing both sides of the law, a man's struggle to know his own true nature, and violence, betrayal and chaos at every turn. Beyond being a show-stopping visual achievement, the six-minute tracking shot is a departure from the established visual style and pacing of *True Detective*.[2] These changes point to the significance of the scene in understanding Rust Cohle's troubled past and whether living as a criminal has corrupted his identity.

> Shiiiiit, just what have you two heard about me?
> — Rust Cohle

Over the course of the nearly twenty-year narrative, Rust Cohle goes from a pessimistic, analytical, and brutally honest loner in 1995 to an older, crankier, pessimistic loner in 2012. There is, however, another version of Cohle lurking in his backstory in the form of his undercover identity, "Crash." In his interview with Detectives Gilbough and Papina, Cohle reveals that he spent four years deep undercover as a "wild man junkie"[3] for the Texas State High Intensity Drug Trafficking Area (H.I.D.T.A). He describes his time undercover using terms more commonly used for prostitution than for police work. "They made me a floater," Cohle says, "a trick,"[4] insinuating that he was exploited by Texas law enforcement, forced to take on dangerous assignments in exchange for the department turning a blind eye to his drug habit. During his time in the H.I.D.T.A., Cohle claims to have killed three cartel men and sustained several gunshot wounds. His wounds were psychological as well as physical, as evidenced by the four months he spent in a psychiatric hospital in Lubbock, Texas.

It's important to note that all Cohle's H.I.D.T.A. files are sealed or classified. He is the only source of information on his experience as Crash and is free to

---

[2] The six-minute tracking shot was almost left on the cutting room floor. Fukunaga discusses the disagreement here: Sharf, Zack. "Cary Fukunaga on the 'Ridiculous' Reason He Exited 'It' and Fighting Nic Pizzolatto to Keep That 'True Detective' Long Take." IndieWire. August 27, 2018. Accessed October 23, 2018.

[3] *True Detective*. "Seeing Things." Episode 2. Directed by Cary Joji Fukunaga. Written by Nic Pizzolatto. HBO. January 19, 2014.

[4] Ibid.

portray his time undercover in any way that he wants. There are no official records that could undermine his story. Cohle could paint himself as a martyr, a victim, or a hero, but he chooses not to apply any moral import to his past. Instead, when talking about his time undercover Cohle grows animated for the first time in the interview. "Street rips, knocking down doors. Within three months I was ripping off couriers or ending up in a Ramada Inn with a couple of fuckin' 8-balls."[5] He describes his undercover experience with urgency and passion, hinting that there is a part of Cohle that enjoyed the chaos and violence of his Crash identity.

> Of course I'm dangerous. I'm police.
> — Rust Cohle

Traditionally, the detective in film noir is not a part of the police force. Sometimes he is a disgraced former cop, but most often he is a private eye, a position which places the detective somewhere between the world of the cops and the world of the criminals. Although Cohle is an official member of the police force (until he quits), his undercover work and subsequent alienation within the force leave him in a role much closer to that of a private eye. He is a part of both worlds, "but at home in neither. He can think like a criminal, but he's on the side of the cops."[6] Being a police detective rather than a private eye also gives Cohle a greater amount of power than the average noir detective. His badge is a shield that grants him access anywhere in the city and protects him from the consequences of his actions. Being able to "do terrible things to people with impunity"[7] is a temptation for any cop, and especially for Cohle, who has been living deep undercover as a criminal.

The noir detective's position leaves him isolated and at times, adrift. In *The Little Sister*, private investigator Phillip Marlowe describes what it feels like to be so deeply immersed in a case that his sense of self begins to fade. "I was a blank man. I had no face, no meaning, no personality, hardly a name... I was the

---

[5] Ibid.

[6] Abrams, Jerold J. "From Sherlock Holmes to the Hard-Boiled Detective in Film Noir." *The Philosophy of Film*.

[7] *True Detective*. "Seeing Things." Episode 2. Directed by Cary Joji Fukunaga. Written by Nic Pizzolatto. HBO. January 19, 2014.

page from yesterday's calendar crumpled at the bottom of the waste basket."[8] For Cohle, this sensation of losing oneself to an investigation is compounded by the fact that he suppressed his identity to become Crash for his undercover work. With no family, no friends within the police department, and no ties within the community, Cohle is at risk of drifting away entirely.

When Cohle joins the Vermilion Parish police force in 1995, he attempts to put his past behind him and live as a functional part of society again. He crafts an ascetic life for himself, sleeping in an unfurnished apartment, refusing to drink with coworkers, and avoiding any social interaction. At this point in the narrative, Cohle's identity is the opposite of his undercover identity. Where Crash thrived in violence and self-gratification, Cohle arrives in Vermilion Parish looking to contribute to society and live an orderly life. To maintain his virtuous identity, Cohle must monitor himself and control his behavior. One example of this self-monitoring occurs after Hart and Cohle nearly come to blows in the precinct locker room. After the confrontation, Cohle lays his fingers on his neck to check his pulse, gauging his physical agitation. Pulse checking is a habit for Cohle, a way of gauging his physical agitation, and an indicator that he is close to losing control of himself.

> Do you ever wonder if you're a bad man?
> — Marty Hart

Cohle's motivation for his isolation and self-monitoring becomes clear during an exchange between Hart and Cohle. Hart, feeling guilty about his infidelity, wonders if he is a bad man. Cohle has no uncertainty on the matter. "No, I don't wonder, Marty. The world needs bad men. We keep other bad men from the door."[9] Where Hart worries that he *might* be a bad man in the context of the choices he makes in his personal life, Cohle sees being good or bad as an absolute state of being, separate from the specific choices or situations.

Cohle also views being bad as a prerequisite for his job. As a detective, he must have contact with criminals and the world of crime. He must be willing to operate on the edges of society, to hurt and kill people when necessary. Being a bad man is part of his job and he is good at his job. In expressing his certainty

---

[8] Chandler, Raymond. *The Little Sister*. New York: Vintage Books, 1988.
[9] *True Detective*. "Who Goes There." Episode 4. Directed by Cary Joji Fukunaga. Written by Nic Pizzolatto. HBO. February 9, 2014.

about being a bad man, Cohle reveals how much of his personal identity is tied to his role as detective. He takes on the "badness" required of him by his job as a personal attribute. He does not say that detectives or police officers must do bad things in order to safeguard society. Cohle says he and Hart are intrinsically bad men.

The timing of this conversation is significant, as it takes place while Hart and Cohle are formulating their plan for Cohle to infiltrate the Iron Crusaders by resurrecting his undercover identity. For Cohle, the idea of becoming Crash again, even for a limited amount of time, is a threat to his new, virtuous identity and the tenuous stability he has carved out in Vermilion Parish. Cohle isolates and monitors himself because he is unsure if he has been so corrupted by his undercover work that he enjoys violence and criminal activity. Cohle may know that he is a bad man, but he still questions what *kind* of bad man he is – is he the type of bad man who "keeps other bad men from the door" or is he the kind of monster that needs to be kept away from society?

> Enough with the self-improvement-penance-hand-wringing shit. Let's go to work.
> — Rust Cohle

Sitting alone in his apartment, Cohle opens a footlocker to reveal guns, grenades, needles and alcohol, all the trappings of his undercover identity. Successfully playing the part of Crash requires that Cohle "embrace the outlaw life."[10] He must wear it like he wears "Crash's" black leather jacket and trust himself to be able to take it off again when he obtains the information he needs. In opening the footlocker, Cohle opens the door for his Crash identity to take over.

Once Cohle makes the decision to use his undercover identity, he becomes a hybrid beast: half undercover lawman and half violent, drug-addled brute. His composite nature is similar to that of the labyrinth-dwelling Minotaur from Greek mythology. Cohle and the Minotaur each represent an unnatural and unstable mix of features contained within a single body; however, he Minotaur's duality is external, Cohle's is internal. More importantly, Cohle is not the victim of fate. He makes a conscious decision to transform himself into an unnatural creature. By agreeing to resurrect his Crash identity, Cohle builds an

---

[10] Ibid.

isolating labyrinth around himself, a maze of conflicting traits, desires, names, and histories that he must navigate in order to stay alive.

> Do I look dead, motherfucker?
> — Crash

The first half of "Who Goes There" sets up Cohle's identity issues, but Cohle does not fully adopt his Crash identity until he meets his contact Ginger at a biker bar. Ginger and other members of the Iron Crusaders believe Crash died in a shootout and are naturally suspicious of his return. Before he agrees to work with Crash, Ginger demands that Crash prove himself as a criminal by snorting an unnamed substance and prove his loyalty to the Iron Crusaders by participating in a raid on a drug stash house in the Hoston projects. Cohle has no choice but to agree. If he backs out, his undercover identity will be blown, as will his ploy to kidnap Ginger and press him for information on the Ledoux brothers and their connection to the Yellow King cult. Ironically, some of the Iron Crusaders plan to wear police uniforms as a disguise when they raid the stash house. The criminals are dressed as cops and Cohle, the undercover cop, is dressed as a criminal. By the time Cohle arrives at the projects, he is juggling multiple identities, motivations, and loyalties.

Rust Cohle, undercover as "Crash," kidnaps Ginger in the Hoston Projects. *True Detective*, season 1, episode 4, "Who Goes There." HBO.

Scenes in the Hoston projects are bookended with aerial shots from the point of view of a police helicopter. From above, the streets of the projects look like pathways in a darkened maze, unevenly lit by the yellow arcs of streetlights. These overhead shots establish the projects as a discrete entity, walled off and separate from the rest of Louisiana and from the rest of the narrative. What happens in the Hoston projects is a trial of character for Cohle. Elements of the projects raid symbolize some of the challenges that Cohle faces as he confronts his true nature. The literal darkness of a nighttime mission represents the darkness that Cohle must face within himself. The mission – stealing drugs from a dealer – replicates the behavior Cohle described when he was out of control and "ripping off couriers."[11] Cohle is using his old undercover identity and committing the same crimes with the same people. The test for Cohle is if he will give into the temptation of violence and degradation that he did in his previous undercover work, or if he will be able to control himself and break the cycle. Though he appears calm when he exits the Iron Crusader's car, Cohle feels the threat and tension of the projects as soon as he hits the streets. Cohle puts his fingers to his throat, checking his pulse and attempting to keep himself under control.

The labyrinthine Hoston projects teem with people, some innocent bystanders and others violent criminals. They crowd into living rooms and kitchens, they fill the streets and they appear as menacing shadows outside the windows of the stash house as Cohle watches the "thirty seconds in and out"[12] plan fall apart before his eyes. The abundance of people adds to the general pandemonium, but it also encourages Cohle to slip deeper into his Crash identity. The people in the projects have no idea Cohle is an undercover cop. To them, he is part of a violent biker gang and they react to him as the threat he appears to be. Every room full of people Cohle encounters while in the Hoston projects is a provocation. Each new face presents him with a dilemma: will he interact with people as "Crash," indiscriminately using brute force, or will he interact with them as Cohle, using only as much violence as necessary for his escape?

---

[11] *True Detective*. "Seeing Things." Episode 2. Directed by Cary Joji Fukunaga. Written by Nic Pizzolatto. HBO. January 19, 2014.
[12] *True Detective*. "Who Goes There." Episode 4. Directed by Cary Joji Fukunaga. Written by Nic Pizzolatto. HBO. February 9, 2014.

The six-minute tracking shot begins just as Cohle enters the projects stash house with Iron Crusaders. At first, Cohle hangs back and lets the gang do the dirty work of beating and intimidation. The Iron Crusaders are bulls in a china shop, bellowing and thrashing at anything that moves, but Cohle remains focused. He performs a textbook sweep of each room of the house as if he were in a police training exercise. When he finds a boy watching T.V., Cohle makes him hide in the bathroom. This isn't necessarily a test of Cohle's character, as he would have to be a complete monster to shoot a child who poses no threat to him. The real challenges come as the atmosphere in the stash house grows claustrophobic as multiple voices shouting threats, demands and refusals blend into a singular roar of anger and fear. The first shot fired[13] by an Iron Crusader is like a starting pistol for Cohle. His multiple identities and motivations boiled down to their most basic element: survival.

Where the rest of *True Detective* utilizes flashbacks, narration, and change of perspective to speed up or slow down the pace of the story, the six-minute tracking shot creates a sense of urgency by portraying Cohle's run through the projects in real time. With all of the time manipulating tricks of filmmaking removed, Cohle's run through the Hoston projects labyrinth is pure forward momentum. Removing the "escape" of cuts and edits becomes a representation of Cohle losing the luxury of weighing the consequences of his actions during his escape. He cannot pause or step away. He can no longer rely on checking his pulse or his other control mechanisms. During the Hoston projects run, Cohle is forced to react without reflection, and in doing so, reveals his true nature.

Faced with one confrontation after another in the six-minute shot, Cohle never uses the gun in his hand. He punches, kicks and grapples, but never uses lethal force. Addled by drugs and adrenaline, he still manages to kidnap Ginger, place a call to Hart, and avoid both the angry inhabitants of the projects as well the police. Cohle escapes the labyrinth of the Hoston projects without falling

---

[13] An enormous support staff was on hand to facilitate filming of the six-minute shot. The special effects make-up required for the scene posed a unique challenge, as there were no cuts between scenes for the make-up team to apply the blood and gore from gunshots after a character was wounded. The solution to this problem was to have make-up artists hide in the scene, then pop out to apply make-up in the few seconds while the camera was focused elsewhere.

prey to the myriad of temptations in his path. Although he used the name "Crash," he never reverted to that unhinged version of himself.

> I know who I am. And after all these years, there's a victory in that.
> — Rust Cohle

Cohle emerges from the Hoston projects having proven to himself that he has not been corrupted by his undercover work. He is cop working undercover as a criminal, not a criminal hiding behind the badge of a cop. It's a small victory, but a victory nonetheless.

Did She Jump or Was She Pushed?: The Making of a Femme Fatale

The final episodes of *True Detective* create a sense of *déjà vu*, as they revisit several of the same scenes and characters which appeared in the 1995 flashback portion of the narrative. This repetition highlights how the characters have changed, or in some cases, how they remain haunted by unanswered questions. The 2012 reunion of Rust Cohle and Maggie Hart in episode seven, "After You've Gone" uses this technique to full effect. While working at the bar, Cohle looks up to see Maggie pull into the parking lot. Cohle does not look directly at Maggie. He watches her approach through a reflection in the mirror behind the bar, a signal that Cohle isn't just noticing Maggie's arrival, he's also reflecting on how she betrayed him by seducing him and using him as a tool to end her marriage. Cohle's face remains impassive, but the lyrics of the song playing in the background of the scene hint at his thoughts. The line "did she jump or was she pushed?" floats through the bar as Cohle ponders what happened between him and his friend's wife. Was Maggie a cold, manipulative woman all along, or was she was pushed to extremes by Hart's cheating and refusal to end their marriage?

Maggie's behavior in *True Detective* marks her as a femme fatale – a woman who uses her sexuality to manipulate and betray men. However,

Maggie doesn't completely fit the femme fatale mold. The femme fatale character is traditionally presented as a habitual deceiver, someone who hides the truth about herself at all costs. In contrast, Maggie's character is defined by her desire for honesty in her relationships with men. This conflict between Maggie's character and her actions is a twist on the traditional femme fatale character, but one that still supports the noir themes in *True Detective* by creating a world where "...questions about the darkness of human nature remain fundamentally unanswered."[1]

> I lay awake thinkin' about women, my daughter, my wife.
> — Rust Cohle

Women in film noir are defined by their relationship to men and can be divided into two main character types: the good woman and the femme fatale. A good woman is traditionally feminine, but not sexual. She is not a threat to the status quo of the noir detective's world because she comfortably fills the role of wife, mother, or helpmate. Her individual desires, sexual or otherwise, are always subjugated to a greater societal good - the same order that the detective is trying to defend from corruption. A good woman's unshakable morality and chastity leaves her out of place in the noir world, limiting her ability to make any significant impact upon it. The good woman can help the detective in a supporting role, often as a dedicated secretary or assistant, but rarely accompanies him on cases or acts of her own volition. Good women mostly end up as victims in the noir world. They are passive objects to be murdered, kidnapped, and raped. Their suffering provides a crime for the detective to investigate, and during the investigation the good woman often becomes a symbol of besmirched purity or innocence rather than a full realized character.

It is worth noting that *True Detective* does not have a good woman as a main character. There are secondary and tertiary characters who could be called good women, characters like the secretary of Vermilion Parish sheriff's office who appears in one scene and helpfully fetches Hart a cup of coffee, Maggie's mother, and Maggie's friend with whom Cohle had a relationship.

---

[1] Abrams, Jerold J. "From Sherlock Holmes to the Hard-Boiled Detective in Film Noir." *The Philosophy of Film Noir*, edited by Mark T. Conard. Lexington: University Press of Kentucky, 2007.

There are few other women in the narrative and most of them are explicitly sexualized. They are prostitutes, like Dora Lange and the other women at the hillbilly bunny ranch, or objects of sexual desire like Hart's girlfriends. Maggie Hart, the femme fatale, is the only adult female with any complexity of character.[2]

Defined by her independence and command of her sexuality, the femme fatale uses sex as a weapon or a tool to control men. The femme fatale's sexuality is threatening not only because she controls it, but also because it exits outside the societally sanctioned bounds of marriage. If she is single, the femme fatale is often promiscuous and if she is married, she is not faithful to her husband. Another common trait of the femme fatale is the rejection of motherhood, a refusal to have children, or once having become a mother, a refusal to raise her children. A femme fatale is constrained by marriage and motherhood, not comfortable. Unlike the good woman, the femme fatale places her personal need for independence above the societal need for stable families and traditional gender roles, making her a threat to society and the status quo.

Maggie Hart's introduction in *True Detective* points to her potential to be a femme fatale. The first scene in which she appears features Maggie lounging in bed, wearing only panties and one of her husband's old shirts. The scene focuses on her body as an object of desire, panning slowly over her curves as her face is turned away from the camera. When she walks down the hallway of her home, she is shot from behind and from the waist down with the focus on the mesmerizing movement of her bare legs. The focus on Maggie's legs should be a huge clue for any viewer familiar with film noir. As critic Janey Place notes, "The femme fatale is characterized by her long lovely legs: our first view of the elusive Velma in *Murder My Sweet* and of Cora in *The Postman Always Rings Twice* is a significant, appreciative shot of their bare legs."[3] Maggie may behave like a good woman in the rest of the scene, dutifully picking up her children's toys and waking her husband with a kiss and a cup of coffee, but the initial shot of her legs tells a different story.

---

[2] Note that Maggie and Marty Hart's daughters are excluded from the list of women in this example. Although they appear as young adults in the final episode, they are children or teens for most of the narrative.

[3] Place, Janey. "Women in Film Noir." In *Women in Film Noir*. London: British Film Institute, 1998.

Lana Turner as leggy femme fatale Cora Smith in a publicity still from *The Postman Always Rings Twice* (Tay Garnett, 1946).

Maggie differs from the traditional femme fatale in that she does not reject motherhood. She has two daughters and genuinely cares for them, making them home cooked meals and tucking them into bed at night. Instead, Maggie's dissatisfaction stems from her restrictive and unsatisfying marriage. She is clearly struggling with her role as Marty Hart's wife even before she learns of his cheating. In episode two, "Seeing Things," Maggie and Marty fight over their contradictory views about what a marriage should be. Hart believes his household should be an oasis of "peace and calm"[4] for him to return to at the end of the day. He wants Maggie to be a subservient good woman, giving him her unquestioning love and support. Whatever happens in her day is inconsequential, "whiny bullshit," and her job is to suppress her personal needs and focus on making her husband comfortable. Marriage, Hart tells his wife, is "supposed to be what *I* want. It's supposed to help *me*."[5]

> Suddenly, you don't own it like you thought you did.
> — Jan (madam, hillbilly bunny ranch)

Men's desire to possess women is a recurring theme in film noir. Women are often treated as prizes to be won or property to be guarded against theft or damage.[6] Marty Hart's attitudes about the women in his life are a textbook example of a man's desire to own women's sexuality. This theme is established early, starting when his girlfriend, Lisa Tragnetti, tries to break off their affair. Hart responds by flying into a jealous rage, kicking down her door and assaulting her new boyfriend. The only question Hart asks Lisa's boyfriend - "Did she suck your dick?"[7] - demonstrates that Hart's main concern is the threat of losing exclusive rights to Lisa's sexuality. Hart's actions also prove that Lisa's desire to end the relationship means nothing to him. The relationship is only over when *he* is ready to relinquish ownership of her body. The theme of owning women's sexuality is made explicit when Hart and Cohle visit the "hillbilly bunny ranch" where Dora Lange once worked. Hart insinuates that the prostitutes are being exploited, but the madam points out his hypocrisy. "Girls walk this Earth all the time screwin' for free. Why is it you add business to the mix and boys like you can't stand the thought?"[8] Hart is not offended that sex is

---

[4] *True Detective*. "Seeing Things." Episode 2. Directed by Cary Joji Fukunaga. Written by Nic Pizzolatto. HBO. January 19, 2014.

[5] Ibid.

[6] Harvey, Sylvia. "Woman's Place: The Absent Family of Film Noir." In *Women in Film Noir*. London: British Film Institute, 1998.

[7] *True Detective*. "The Locked Room." Episode 3. Directed by Cary Joji Fukunaga. Written by Nic Pizzolatto. HBO. January 26, 2014.

[8] *True Detective*. "Seeing Things." Episode 2. Directed by Cary Joji Fukunaga. Written by Nic Pizzolatto. HBO. January 19, 2014.

being sold – he is offended that women at the ranch are in control, using their sexuality as a tool to turn a profit.

Hart's attitude toward women's sexuality extends to Maggie as well. As a faithful wife, Maggie's sexuality is no longer her own – she can express it only with her husband. Hart, however, does not seem to have any interest in meeting Maggie's sexual needs. Hart's neglect of Maggie's needs echoes the loveless dynamic of many femme fatale's marriages in film noir. In *Double Indemnity*, Phyllis Dietrichson (played by Barbara Stanwyk) feels trapped in her marriage and her husband's home. She justifies plotting his murder by explaining that he has no affection for her, only indifference. "I feel as if he was watching me. Not that he cares, not *anymore*. But he keeps me on a leash so tight I can't breathe."[9]

Marty Hart exhibits the same jealous behavior as Phyllis Dietrichson's husband, trying to control Maggie's sexuality while having no interest in satisfying her himself. This is illustrated in the scene where Cohle does some yard work for Maggie. After completing his task, Cohle sits in the Hart family kitchen, sweaty and stripped down to his undershirt. There is nothing inappropriate in the text of Cohle and Maggie's conversation, but Maggie exudes sexual energy in the scene, coming up to, but not crossing the line into outright flirting. Hart returns home to this scene and responds with predictable jealousy. Hart claims to like "mowing his lawn,"[10] in a thinly veiled metaphor for having sex with his wife, but her behavior makes it clear he has not been keeping up with the job. Hart barks "don't ever mow my lawn,"[11] at Cohle while standing next to a bin overflowing with bright green grass clippings, a symbol of Maggie's mounting unmet sexual needs.

> It's hard to admit defeat.
> — Maggie Hart

Maggie's sexual frustration and dissatisfaction with her marriage are in line with the femme fatale character, but her reticence to leave her marriage is not.

---

[9] *Double Indemnity*, Directed by Billy Wilder, 1944.
[10] *True Detective*. "The Locked Room." Episode 3. Directed by Cary Joji Fukunaga. Written by Nic Pizzolatto. HBO. January 26, 2014.
[11] *True Detective*. "Who Goes There." Episode 4. Directed by Cary Joji Fukunaga. Written by Nic Pizzolatto. HBO. February 9, 2014.

Maggie is betrayed by both Hart and Cohle before she resorts to using her sexuality as a weapon.

Maggie Hart on date night. *True Detective*, season 1, episode 3, "The Locked Room." HBO.

Although it seems rather obvious, Maggie struggles to figure out what is wrong with her marriage in the early portion of the narrative. In the confines of their bedroom, Maggie questions her husband, hoping to confront their issues head on. The best answer Maggie can get out of Hart is an admission that he is "all fucked up,"[12] which is not new information for her. During the same period, Maggie reaches out to Cohle when Hart fails to come home on time. Instead of telling Maggie the truth, Cohle protects his partner with lies. In both instances, Maggie came to a man in her life asking for the truth and was deliberately deceived.

After learning of Hart's infidelity, Maggie attempts to separate from her husband but is not successful for reasons that were foreshadowed in Hart's violent reaction to losing his girlfriend. Maggie taking the children, moving to her parent's house, and cutting off all contact with him isn't enough to convince

---

[12] *True Detective*. "The Locked Room." Episode 3. Directed by Cary Joji Fukunaga. Written by Nic Pizzolatto. HBO. January 26, 2014.

Hart that his marriage is over. Instead of accepting his situation, Hart confronts Maggie at her workplace, causing a scene. As he is dragged away by Cohle, Hart says to his wife, "I love you honey. I ain't giving up."[13] With his history of controlling behavior, Marty's parting words sound less like a declaration of love and more like a threat that he will never give up his hold over Maggie.

During her separation from Hart, Cohle betrays once Maggie again. Forced to play the go-between, Cohle meets Maggie at a diner. He skips passing along Hart's apologies and moves straight to advising Maggie to reconcile with Hart, "Men, women... it's not supposed to work, except to make kids. It's not about you."[14] In doing so, Cohle reduces Maggie to her role as a mother. He negates her existence as an independent human being with a need for love, sex, and agency over her own life. Maggie's needs do not matter to Cohle as much as maintaining the status quo for the good of society. All Maggie can do is marvel at the hypocrisy in Cohle's advice and express her disgust. "So, at the end of the day you duck under rationalization, same as any of them."[15]

Realizing that she cannot leave until Hart is ready to let her go, Maggie begins the reconciliation process with her husband. Maggie does not have the voice to express her own hopelessness, but everything else about the scene at the roller rink evokes a sense of being trapped in a hopeless cycle, from the skaters tracing laps around the flat circle of the rink to the Kink's *Tired of Waiting for You* playing in the background. Being a good woman and playing by society's rules leaves Maggie trapped in an unhealthy marriage, but given the femme fatale elements of her character, Maggie will not be trapped forever.

> In a former life I used to exhaust myself navigating crude men who thought they were clever.
> — Maggie Hart

Episode six, "Haunted Houses" marks a turning point in the narrative. In earlier episodes, the 2012 interviews focus on Hart and Cohle. Their commentary provides context for the flashback scenes and serves as a version

---

[13] Ibid.

[14] *True Detective*. "Who Goes There." Episode 4. Directed by Cary Joji Fukunaga. Written by Nic Pizzolatto. HBO. February 9, 2014.

[15] Ibid.

of the voice-over narration common in film noir.[16] In the sixth episode, Hart and Cohle are no longer talking to Gilbough and Papina. Instead, Maggie sits down for an interview, changing the context for her actions by adding her point of view to the narrative for the first time.

In another major shift, the Maggie that Detectives Gilbough and Papina meet is a very different woman than the Maggie Hart who appears in the flashbacks. Younger Maggie favored floral dresses, blue jeans and big hair. In 2012, Maggie enters the interview looking polished in a simple green blouse and gold necklace. She exudes confidence, poise, and intelligence. Unlike Hart and Cohle, who allowed the interviewers to set the pace of conversation, Maggie wastes no time in asking Gilbough and Papina, "What are you looking for from me?"[17] She also sets her own terms for the interview, telling the detectives, "ask your questions or I'm leaving."[18] This Maggie is clearly not the same woman who acted against her own best interest and stayed in a doomed marriage. She sounds and acts more like a femme fatale - cool, calculating, and in control.

> This will hurt him.
> — Maggie Hart

Episode six features an interrogation scene which foreshadows Maggie's betrayal of Hart and Cohle. In the scene, Cohle interrogates the "Marshland Medea," a woman accused of killing her children. Best known by the eponymous ancient Greek Tragedy by Euripides, Medea is a barbarian who aided Jason and his Argonauts with her wits and witchcraft. After their adventures were over, Jason married Medea and fathered her children. When Jason failed to remain faithful, Medea exacted a calculated revenge by killing their sons. She killed her children, not because they did anything wrong, but because she believed it was the best way to hurt her husband.[19] Much like the

---

[16] Hirsch, Foster. *The Dark Side of the Screen: Film Noir*. Cambridge, MA: Da Capo Press, 2008.
[17] *True Detective*. "Haunted Houses." Episode 6. Directed by Cary Joji Fukunaga. Written by Nic Pizzolatto. HBO. February 23, 2014.
[18] Ibid.
[19] Euripides. *Medea*. Mineola, NY: Dover., 1993. "**Chorus:** But can you have the heart to kill your flesh and blood? **Medea:** Yes, for it is the best way to wound my husband."

femme fatale character, Medea is interpreted by critics as both a proto-feminist figure and as a misogynistic reaction to a powerful woman.

Maggie's betrayal, like Medea's, is cold and calculated. It is executed with the twin goals of ending her marriage and hurting her husband as much as possible. When Maggie seduces Cohle, she is fighting for a chance to break free of her unhappy marriage and she's willing to do it using the only weapon she has – her sexuality.

Mirroring her actions in the earlier portion of the narrative, Maggie goes to Cohle when she learns of Hart's cheating. This time around, she doesn't phone him or meet him in a public place. In a classic femme fatale move, she shows up at his door in tears, begging for help. Surprised, Cohle lets her in and mentions that he's off the Yellow King cult investigation, despite the crime scene photos littering his home. In a sense, Cohle and Maggie are both "off the job" – Cohle is pursuing an investigation without departmental support and Maggie is leaving behind her roles of wife and mother to get answers of her own. When acting as a femme fatale, Maggie doesn't want answers about her husband – she needs answers for herself. Instead of asking Cohle, she tells him, "be honest with me now."[20] She is counting on her sexuality to force a confession of sorts from Cohle. If he is attracted to her, he will not be able to resist her advances.

Maggie is clearly the aggressor in this scenario, closing in like a predator as Cohle averts his gaze and leans away. When Cohle gives into Maggie's seduction, their desire results in sex that is as cold as the stark white backdrop of Cohle's kitchen. Maggie's body remains covered by her dress during the sex scene, indicating that she is still somewhat in control, but Cohle is exposed from the waist down, highlighting naked lust driving his actions. Maggie and Cohle do not look at each other during sex, indicating that although they are joined physically, they are mentally and emotionally disconnected. This separation is reinforced in a closeup shot that focuses on Maggie's astonished expression, leaving Cohle as a blurry shape over her shoulder. The focus on Maggie's face highlights the emotional significance this event holds for her. She may have had the potential to be a femme fatale, but successfully seducing Cohle proves that after seventeen years of a neglectful marriage, Maggie still knows how to wield her sexuality.

---

[20] *True Detective*. "Haunted Houses." Episode 6. Directed by Cary Joji Fukunaga. Written by Nic Pizzolatto. HBO. February 23, 2014.

After the act, Maggie is the first to pull away, gently removing Cohle's hand from her waist. Cohle, the skilled interrogator and master judge of character is stunned by Maggie's hidden sexual power, as well as her willingness to use it against the men in her life. Cohle's shock and disgust mirrors Maggie's reaction when he advised her to reunite with her cheating husband. In using Cohle as the tool for her infidelity, Maggie betrays Cohle in the same way he betrayed her – she reduces him to his gender and his role. She used Cohle as man and she used his role as Hart's partner to make her infidelity more painful to her husband. Just as Cohle ignored Maggie's individual needs in the earlier portion of the narrative, Maggie ignores the detrimental impacts her actions will have on Cohle's life, his job, and his relationship with Hart. However, even in her moment of betrayal Maggie isn't completely cold. Her parting words to Cohle are, "I'm sorry, but thank you."[21]

Seducing Cohle is the point where Maggie becomes a femme fatale and the point at which she takes control of her life. It is a transformative event, as marked by the blocking of the scene. Maggie enters Cohle's house through the front door as a respectable woman, someone whom Cohle trusts and accepts into his home. Maggie leaves his house through the back door of the house, one just off the kitchen. She leaves as a betrayer, a femme fatale who cannot be trusted.

Having proven herself a femme fatale, Maggie has the power to confront Hart and shake his control over her. Since Hart does not recognize a woman's right to own her body and her sexuality, he would never respect Maggie's decision to leave him. In Hart's view, a woman has no right to leave until he is done with her. However, since Hart recognizes a man's claim to a woman's body, Maggie figured out she could break his hold by giving herself to another man. Maggie used Cohle as a tool to usurp Hart's ownership of her sexuality. In doing so, she betrayed both men, but not with lies or deception. She simply found a flaw in their understanding of women and used it against them.

> Now, get on out of here. You're classing the place up.
> — Marty Hart

Seeing Maggie only in the context of her role as wife and mother means Hart and Cohle never really understand her. It is the men's inability to see

---

[21] Ibid.

Maggie as an individual that drives her to betray them. This lack of understanding also creates the blind spot that Maggie exploits to free herself – both men refused to listen to Maggie's needs and therefore they never knew what she was capable of in the extremes of her desperation.

This fundamental misunderstanding is repeated in the 2012 scene where Maggie visits Cohle at the bar. She asks Cohle to tell her that whatever they're up to is not something that's going to get Hart hurt. Cohle hears this request and assumes Maggie is asking to be comforted with a lie. "It never sat right with me then and it doesn't now," he replies, "you asking me to lie to you about him."[22] As a jaded cop, Cohle lives in a world of lies and deception. He never considers that Maggie is an honest person, and as such wants a truthful answer. Throughout the narrative Maggie never asked Cohle to lie about Hart's cheating. She asked him for the truth, for the confirmation she needed to get out of her unhappy marriage. Instead, Cohle patronized her with lies.

Despite knowing her, Detectives Hart and Cohle cannot understand Maggie because they only see her in terms of her gender. Hart needs Maggie to be a chaste, maternal, "good woman," and is unwilling to see her as an individual with her own needs and sexuality. Similarly, Cohle defines Maggie by her role as Hart's wife and mother to Hart's children. Both men fail to see Maggie as a person and thus can never understand her motivation for betraying them. Since *True Detective* is told mainly through the perspectives of Hart and Cohle, the narrative ends with no clear answer as to whether Maggie was a cold femme fatale all along, or if she was pushed into it by the habitual deception from the men in her life.

---

[22] *True Detective.* "After You've Gone." Episode 7. Directed by Cary Joji Fukunaga. Written by Nic Pizzolatto. HBO. March 2, 2014.

It's a Family Thing: Southern Gothic in *True Detective*

Set amid the moss-draped cypress trees of bayou country, Southern gothic is a uniquely American genre. It began as an offshoot of gothic fiction, transplanting darkly romantic themes from remote English moors to isolated communities in the rural South of the United States. The distinction between the two genres is more than geographical. Southern gothic has a stronger focus on social commentary, particularly on the detrimental impacts of corruption, poverty, and racism on rural Americans. Illustrating the full impact of these issues can be difficult, as they are a result of complex, long standing social and economic factors. Rather than tackling these issues directly, Southern gothic writers take an oblique approach by employing horror tropes common to gothic fiction, primarily a "fixation on the grotesque, and a tension between realistic and supernatural events."[1] Using taboo imagery in this way transforms complex problems into visceral horrors which are impossible to ignore. In *True Detective*, writer Nic Pizzolatto and director Cary Joji Fukunaga follow this tradition, using eerie and grotesque imagery to illustrate how predatory organizations like the Tuttle ministries corrupt the disadvantaged communities they claim to help.

---

[1] Marshall, Bridget. "Defining Southern Gothic." In *Critical Insights: Southern Gothic Literature.* Vol. 1. Salem Press, 2013.

What do you know about Sam Tuttle? All the branches of the Tuttle family?
— Marty Hart

Pizzolatto and Fukunaga foreshadow the importance of the Tuttle family tree early in the narrative by including a tree in the scene where Dora Lange's body is discovered. Although the tree appears strong and healthy, everything in its shadow is destroyed, from the charred remains of a sugar cane crop to the violated corpse of a young woman. When Detectives Hart and Cohle arrive on the scene, they focus on the desecration of Dora's body and the occult imagery associated with her death. Their focus on the tawdriest elements of the murder scene results in Hart and Cohle falling victim to the "detective's curse," unable to see the clue that is right under their nose. To catch her killer, the detectives must look beyond the murdered woman. They must examine the society in which she lived, namely Vermilion Parish where the Tuttle family tree has been central to the community for "a long, long time."[2]

From the outside, the Tuttle family appears to be a pillar of social responsibility. Reverend Billy Lee Tuttle is the first family member to appear onscreen and he serves as the central representative of the powerful clan. At the outset of the narrative, Reverend Tuttle arrives in the sheriff's office unannounced and lobbies for the Lange murder case to be handled by a special task force. Ostensibly the Reverend acts out of concern for his flock, but his visit is also a none too subtle reminder of the power his family wields in Vermilion Parish. Usually private citizens are not allowed to dictate the course of a police investigation. The Tuttle clan, however, has members in political and government positions across the state of Louisiana, which explains why the police are so accommodating of the Reverend's requests. The Tuttle family also exerts influence over the community through their "charitable organizations and educational initiatives."[3] In doing so they brand themselves as public servants, linking the Tuttle family name with generosity and the greater good. This tactic puts the Tuttle family beyond reproach. They are so enmeshed with

---

[2] *True Detective*. "After You've Gone." Episode 7. Directed by Cary Joji Fukunaga. Written by Nic Pizzolatto. HBO. March 2, 2014.
[3] *True Detective*. "Haunted Houses." Episode 6. Directed by Cary Joji Fukunaga. Written by Nic Pizzolatto. HBO. February 23, 2014.

the community that to question the motivations of the Tuttle family is to cast aspersion on the moral fiber of Vermilion Parish as a whole.

Like the dynastic families in many Southern gothic tales, the Tuttle family is large and complex. In the course of their investigation, Detectives Hart and Cohle learn that patriarch Sam Tuttle was a licentious man who, "... has lots of children. All types."[4] By fathering children in and out of wedlock, Sam Tuttle corrupted the integrity of his family, splitting it into two branches: the upstanding branch of the family, composed of powerful upper-class characters like Reverend Tuttle, and the corrupted branch, composed of lower class characters descended from Sam Tuttle's illegitimate children. Denied the family name and cut off from the family wealth and privilege, the offspring on the corrupted branch grow further and further apart from what made the Tuttle family great. The result is a grotesque character like Errol Childress, a degenerate caricature of his upstanding relatives.

In a different genre, the bifurcated Tuttle family tree might be used to set up a dichotomy between the goodness and purity of the upper class Tuttles and the ghastly immorality of the illegitimate Tuttles. In Southern gothic, however, the emphasis is on how both branches of the Tuttle family are corrupt and grotesque. The two branches of the Tuttle family may seem like complete opposites, but they are inexorably linked by a sinister tradition of occult worship.

> Thank you, we're very proud of our ministries.
> — Reverend Billy Tuttle

When rumors surface of child molestation at the Tuttle-sponsored Wellspring schools, Cohle pays Reverend Billy Lee Tuttle a visit at the Tuttle Ministry headquarters. With clean, modern architecture, manicured lawns and fresh-faced students, the Tuttle campus appears utopian, a vision of what rural Louisiana could become with actual investment in the community. The idea behind the Wellspring program sounds equally appealing. Tuttle ministries accepted school vouchers as payment for private school tuition for underprivileged children. However, instead of providing kids with education and spiritual guidance, the Tuttles used the program to identify children who

---

[4] *True Detective*. "After You've Gone." Episode 7. Directed by Cary Joji Fukunaga. Written by Nic Pizzolatto. HBO. March 2, 2014.

are most likely to fall through the cracks in society and target them for molestation.

The Tuttle family's scheme is a misappropriation of public funds and betrayal of parents who only want the best for their children. It is a grotesque mockery of the aid that education and religion are supposed to provide to poor communities. It is not, however, a fictional problem. Many families in rural America struggle to find adequate education for their children. Inadequate funding, difficulty in attracting qualified faculty, and poor technological infrastructure are just a few of the myriad issues driving the lack of educational opportunities for rural children. School vouchers are a commonly proposed solution, but they offer mixed results.[5] Currently there is no clear answer to how to fix this problem, but there are unscrupulous people who, like the Tuttles, see an opportunity to extract a profit from these already disadvantaged communities.

From a creative standpoint, the problem of rural education doesn't lend itself to an emotionally compelling narrative. While there are very real human dramas and suffering caused by this problem, they often happen slowly and over a long period of time. It is difficult to dramatize the economic impact that poor education, a lack of jobs, or lack of skilled workers can have on a community. This is where the grotesque and supernatural elements of Southern gothic can illustrate the detrimental impacts of real world corruption better than a strictly factual representation.

The grotesque images in *True Detective* represent the symptoms of the Tuttle family's corrupting influence in the community. As Rust Cohle and Marty Hart investigate Dora Lange's murder, they find that each person they interview had a family member in the Wellspring school program and has some visible physical malady. Dora Lange's mother suffers from terrible headaches, tremors, and gnarled hands. The tent revival church that Dora briefly attended is full of parishioners who are sick, elderly, or mentally challenged. Marie Fontenot's uncle Danny, once a star athlete, is so debilitated from a series of strokes that

---

[5] Mills, Jonathan N., and Patrick J. Wolf. "HOW HAS THE LOUISIANA SCHOLARSHIP PROGRAM AFFECTED STUDENTS? A Comprehensive Summary of Effects after Three Years." Education Research Alliance for New Orleans. June 26, 2017. Accessed October 07, 2018. https://educationresearchalliancenola.org/files/publications/ERA1706-Policy-Brief-Louisiana-Scholarship-Program-EMBARGOED-170626.pdf.

he can no longer communicate. During the scenes in the Fontenot household, director Cary Joji Fukunaga builds a claustrophobic atmosphere by focusing on Danny Fontenot as he tries to speak. Watching the man struggle, grow agitated, and finally be ignored is deeply uncomfortable. It elicits feelings of terror at the frailty of the human body and shame at the revulsion or annoyance felt when forced to look at a body that is failing. The overall effect is grotesque, eliciting a visceral reaction to the Fontenot family's losses.

The Tuttle family's worship of the Yellow King cult ties into the theme of corruption, as it is a depraved version of spirituality that calls for blood sacrifice. It highlights the Tuttle family's exploitation of their role as spiritual leaders and their betrayal of a community's trust. The eerie and supernatural imagery Pizzolatto and Fukunaga use in association with the Yellow King, however, performs a different function than the physical grotesques used in other parts of the narrative. Where the grotesque forces the audience to engage emotionally by focusing on unpleasant images, the supernatural imagery is a substitution for images too heinous to be displayed. In *True Detective*, supernatural imagery serves as a stand-in for evidence of the sexual molestation of children.

In episode seven, "Since You Were Gone," Cohle reveals that he has a stolen video tape proving the Tuttle family's ritual abuse and murder of children. Cohle describes it as "a very rural sense of Mardi Gras —you know, men on horses, animal masks and such." He goes on to say that they also have a "winter festival, heavy on the Saturnalia, a place where Santeria and voodoo got all meshed together."[6] This description sets up an expectation of something sinister and unnatural. Photographs of the child in the video show her standing alone in the woods with a blindfold over her eyes and a crown of antlers on her head. She looks small, lost, and terribly vulnerable. Using the imagery of occult worship evokes the child's sense of fear and helplessness, without showing any of the despicable acts to which she was subjected. This allows the creators to tell a compelling story about corrupt adults who abuse power and hurt children, but does so in a way that doesn't completely repulse the audience.

Pizzolatto and Fukunaga use a combination of grotesque and supernatural imagery to paint a full picture of the depravity of the Tuttle family and the

---

[6] *True Detective*. "After You've Gone." Episode 7. Directed by Cary Joji Fukunaga. Written by Nic Pizzolatto. HBO. March 2, 2014.

damage their social programs caused. Rather than being a source of financial and spiritual support, the Tuttle family is a parasite, sucking the vitality out of the community around them. The Wellspring program is aptly named, as the children of Vermilion Parish are a bountiful resource for the Tuttle family. They treat these children like livestock, taking them from their parents and grooming them in the Wellspring schools until they are ready to be consumed. Sentient meat to be sacrificed at the altar of the Yellow King.

> You know what they did to me? What I will do to all the sons and daughters of man.
> — Errol Childress

Errol Childress remains shrouded in mystery until the final episode of *True Detective*. The episode opens with a view into Childress's daily life and it is pure Southern gothic grotesque. Rising from the swamps, the Childress home is a faded plantation house surrounded by shacks that were once slave cabins - a potent visual reminder of the Tuttle family's long history of exploitation and cruelty. Childress's immediate family is even more appalling. His "daddy" is a flyblown corpse strapped to a bed and his mentally challenged relative (half-sister or cousin) Betty is also his lover.

It's not an accident that that the most grotesque and supernatural imagery in the narrative centers around Errol Childress. He is the point of convergence for all the Southern gothic corruption in the narrative. He is not just touched by the corrupting influence of the Tuttle family; he is the product of it and a perpetrator of it in his own right. An important clue to Childress's motivation comes from his name. Childress is Old English and was either an occupational name for a family that ran an orphanage, or a name given to an orphaned or unwanted child.[7] Though he is not an orphan, Childress is from the corrupted branch of the Tuttle family. He is not granted the family name and certainly not acknowledged by respectable family members like Reverend Tuttle. In giving Errol the last name Childress, Nic Pizzolatto highlights the key conflict in the character. Despite being shunned, Childress still identifies with the Tuttle family.

---

[7] Hanks, Patrick, ed. *Dictionary of American Family Names: Volume 1 A-F*. New York: Oxford Press, 2003.

Childress is willing to do anything to feel closer to the family that has rejected him. In a scene that plays the most loathsome elements of Southern gothic for shock value, Childress molests Betty. "Tell me about grandpa,"[8] he says, cooing as Betty retells the story of their grandfather raping her as a child. Childress's sexual relationship with his female relative (unclear if she is a half-sister or cousin) emulates his grandfather's wanton behavior. It allows him to feel connected to his grandfather, as they have had sex with the same woman. It also illustrates that his depravity is not an aberration in the larger Tuttle family. By molesting his sister, he is copying the behavior of his grandfather and carrying on a Tuttle family tradition.

Errol Childress and his relative Betty engage in an incestuous relationship and live in the decaying remnants of a once grand house. *True Detective*, season 1, episode 8, "Form and Void." HBO.

There are clues in the narrative that Errol Childress and his cousins, Reggie and Dewall Ledoux, were victims of ritual molestation as children. Like other victims of the Yellow King cult, the men are branded or tattooed with a spiral. When Cohle chases Childress into the crumbling tunnels of Carcosa, Childress gives a rambling sermon about his spiritual journey. In it he mentions his cousins, saying, "blessed Reggie, Dewall, acolytes, witnesses to my journey.

---

[8] *True Detective*. "Form and Void." Episode 8. Directed by Cary Joji Fukunaga. Written by Nic Pizzolatto. HBO. March 9, 2014.

Lovers. I am not ashamed."[9] Given the amoral behavior of the upper-class Tuttles, it makes sense that they would have no problem with using children from the illegitimate branch of the family for ritual abuse. If Childress and the Ledoux brothers were used in occult ceremonies as children, it would explain how they gleaned some knowledge of the signs and symbols associated with the Yellow King.

Errol Childress's killings are his attempts to imitate the ritual sacrifices he saw performed as a child. The murders are Childress's "very important work,"[10] an aggrandizement that justifies his vision of himself as part of the greater Tuttle clan. His killings, however, are a corruption of the carefully engineered upper-class Tuttle family sacrifices. The entire Wellspring schools program was created to identify and groom potential victims. Though depraved, the upper-class sacrifices are discreet, leaving behind no corpses to raise questions. In contrast, Childress murders Dora Lange and stages her body in public with imagery that ties the crime back to the upstanding branch of the Tuttle family. Placing her body at the foot of a large tree, rather than at his altar to the Yellow King, Childress seems to be sacrificing Dora to the upper-class branch of his family rather than to a supernatural being. Read in this context, the murder of Dora is Childress's perverse plea for acceptance by the upper-class Tuttles. Despite being a victim of their molestation and neglect, he is still desperate for their approval.

Ultimately, Childress's wish to serve the larger Tuttle family is granted. When Hart and Cohle's investigation into the Yellow King cult murders closes in on the respectable branch of the Tuttle family, they sacrifice Errol one last time, using the sad and grotesque reality of his life as a distraction from the ongoing crimes and corruption of the larger Tuttle family. In the final episode, footage from a news broadcast shows titillating footage of police investigators unearthing human remains on the Childress property. Almost as an afterthought, a newscaster assures the viewing audience that, "the state Attorney General and the F.B.I. have discredited rumors that the accused was in some way related to Louisiana Senator, Edwin Tuttle."[11]

---

[9] Ibid.
[10] Ibid.
[11] Ibid.

My family's been here a long, long time.
   — Errol Childress

Southern gothic is a delicate balancing act, a push and pull of shocking an audience with some grotesque imagery and offering a supernatural substitute for the images that are too horrible to be portrayed. Grotesque imagery is a powerful storytelling tool that can, when used injudiciously, be exploitative rather than illustrative. However, when done well it becomes a tool to illustrate the impacts of complex, longstanding social issues. In *True Detective*, Southern gothic elements allow Pizzolatto and Fukunaga to expose how the upper-class members of the Tuttle family prey on the lower classes of Vermilion Parish, and how the lower classes still look to the corrupt upper-class Tuttles for charity and spiritual guidance. The grotesque and supernatural images in the narrative are visible symptoms of the corruption that the Tuttle family has kept hidden for a long, long time.

The Stories We Tell Ourselves: The Role of Religion in Shaping Reality

Christianity and Christian religious imagery are recurring motifs in *True Detective*. This is in keeping with Southern gothic tradition, as is the inclusion of a contrasting occult or folk magic element. This juxtaposition between Christianity and occult spirituality allows for an exploration of the power of religion and the influential role it plays in Southern communities. Nic Pizzolatto takes a novel approach to the use of religious themes by introducing a third belief system to the narrative. Rust Cohle's "flat circle" interpretation of string theory is not a religion *per se*, as he does not believe in a god, but when compared with Evangelical Christianity and the Yellow King cult, the similarities between Cohle's beliefs and the other two religions become clear. All three belief systems tell a story about a hidden reality outside the boundaries of human perception and how suffering and death are the keys to entering that unseen realm.

> I'm here today to talk to you about reality.
> — Joel Theriot

The Friends of Christ tent revival scene highlights the importance religion has in shaping reality in the narrative. Preacher Joel Theriot's passionate sermon serves as the central text outlining religion's ability to define reality. He begins by telling his audience "this... is not real."[1] While gesturing at the tangible world around him, he explains that everything commonly accepted as reality "is merely the limitation of our senses..." Theriot goes one step further, portraying physical existence as a cage and humans as "...prisoners of light and matter."[2] Theriot's argument that the physical world is a prison presupposes a world outside of the cage – a world other than physical reality, beyond what can be seen or verified.

Theriot's description of a dual reality draws from the Christian Gospel. Also known as the "Good News," the Gospel is a message of hope. It states that although life in the physical world may be full of sorrow, people should rejoice because the Kingdom of God is near.[3] Upon their death, true believers can be delivered from the cage of their bodies to enjoy an existence free from all suffering in the Kingdom of God. This permeability between the physical world and the spiritual world is made possible by the death and resurrection of Jesus Christ, an act which absolved men of their sin and reconciled man and God. The "Good News" is that through Christ's sacrifice, entrance to the Kingdom of God is possible for believers. All who accept Christ as their savior can endure hardship knowing they will enjoy spiritual reward after death.

The idea of a life after death in a non-physical realm is common to many world religions. It is so familiar, in fact, that it is easy to overlook the fantastical elements of the premise. This is where the introduction of occult spirituality proves essential to the Southern gothic story. Presenting an unfamiliar religion invites the audience to question the tenets of the new religion and in turn, contrast it with some the core beliefs of Christianity.

In *True Detective*, the Yellow King cult is introduced as the opposite of the Evangelical Christianity practiced in Vermilion Parish. While Christianity is practiced openly, worship of the Yellow King happens in the shadows. Christians like Marty Hart are proud of their religion and extol its virtuous influence on society. In contrast, the Yellow King cult is introduced in connection with a murder, an act which is inherently threatening to civil society.

---

[1] *True Detective*. "The Locked Room." Episode 3. Directed by Cary Joji Fukunaga. Written by Nic Pizzolatto. HBO. January 26, 2014.
[2] Ibid.
[3] Mark 1:14 – 15. In *Holy Bible: NRSV, New Revised Standard Version*. New York: Harper Bibles, 2007.

Cloaked in mystery, the cult is so elusive that the detectives struggle to find hard proof of its existence. The secrecy surrounding the cult makes a direct comparison to Christianity difficult, as there is no holy book or sermon to spell out the Yellow King doctrine. Failing an official source, members of the Yellow King cult serve as the conduits of the core beliefs of their faith, revealing surprising similarities between their worldview and Christianity.

During the raid on the Ledoux compound, cultist Reggie Ledoux's ominous rambling hints at a belief in a world outside the physical plane of existence. Cohle points a gun at Ledoux, pushing the boundary between life and death, creating a moment in time where the physical and spiritual worlds collide. Ledoux is oddly unconcerned with the prospect of his imminent death. He looks to the sky and whispers, "black stars rise,"[4] as if he is seeing through the blue sky above him and into a different reality. As established in Dora Lange's diary, black stars are symbols associated with the lost city of Carcosa where members of the cult believe that the Yellow King dwells. "He sees you,"[5] Ledoux tells Cohle, invoking the Yellow King and echoing Joel Theriot's sermon, which used the same words to remind his audience that a Christian god was looking down on the physical realm from heaven.

Ledoux's calm demeanor during the raid suggests he is prepared for death. "It's time" he says to Cohle, "I know what happens next."[6] His repetition of the words "black stars" and "Carcosa" become a prayer uttered in anticipation of his release from the cage of physical existence. Although he is not dead yet, Ledoux is close enough to see the Yellow King cult's spiritual realm and anticipate his arrival in that promised land. In this way, Ledoux's religious ecstasy is like the peace a Christian might experience upon viewing the pearly gates of the Kingdom of God when facing his own mortality. Joel Theriot and Reggie Ledoux both take solace in the notion of a spiritual realm outside the physical world, but belief in the existence of an unseen realm, be it the Kingdom of God or the lost city of Carcosa, requires a certain willingness to set aside reason in favor of faith.

---

[4] *True Detective.* "The Secret Fate of All Life." Episode 5. Directed by Cary Joji Fukunaga. Written by Nic Pizzolatto. HBO. February 16, 2014
[5] Ibid.
[6] Ibid.

Religion is a language virus that rewrites pathways in the brain. Dulls critical thinking.
— Rust Cohle

Standing at the back of the Friends of Christ tent revival, Cohle observes that Theriot's congregation is filled with impoverished Southerners with "a yen for fairy tales."[7] Cohle's assessment is harsh, but it is also true that Theriot's congregation is composed of the tired, the sick, the aged, the addicted, and the feeble. These are the faces of rural poverty, of people who are used up, tossed away and forgotten when a factory closes or an industry moves offshore. They are people desperate for good news, as the world around them gives them little reason to believe their lives will get better any time soon.

Cohle views the congregation with distain, but Theriot, as a man of God, sees their desperation as an opportunity to share the Good News. He uses his showmanship and impassioned rhetoric to increase his audience's capacity for illusion. Although Theriot's evangelism is altruistic, he still uses his congregation's hope to manipulate them into believing the fantastical idea of a life after death. Using the metaphor of religion as a "language virus," Theriot can be seen as the vector of infection, injecting the virus of religion into the minds of his rapt audience. In doing so, he eases their pain but also weakens their ability to tell fantasy from reality, making them more susceptible to infection by other mind contagions peddled by other storytellers with less benign motives.

Theriot's congregation are easy targets for religious conversion. This fact does not escape Errol Childress, who uses the Friends of Christ revival as an opportunity to evangelize for his religion. Like Christianity, the Yellow King cult offers the promise of life after death, only the eternal reward is redeemed in Carcosa rather than in the Kingdom of Heaven. Both realms are unseen and unverifiable. Their existence is predicated in desperation on the part of the faithful. This need is then harnessed by a preacher, who "absorbs their [the parishioner's] dread with his narrative."[8] The names are different, but the story is the same. Be it Christianity or the Yellow King, it's the same fairy tale that was

---

[7] *True Detective*. "The Locked Room." Episode 3. Directed by Cary Joji Fukunaga. Written by Nic Pizzolatto. HBO. January 26, 2014.
[8] Ibid.

used to lure in Dora Lange, a "torn-up person on her last legs,"[9] with the promise of an end to her suffering.

> You ever hear of something called M-brane theory, Detectives?
> — Rust Cohle

Religion does not have a monopoly on positing the existence of unseen worlds. Theoretical physics is a scientific field that uses mathematical models, mainstream theories and abstractions to predict the existence of natural phenomena that have never been observed. The M-brane theory that Cohle mentions in his interview with Detectives Gilbough and Papina is an untested theory in this field.

In simple terms, M-brane can be described as a theory about the shape and substance of the universe.[10] The existence of such a theory was first posited by theoretical physicist Edward Witten at a string theory conference in 1995. According to Witten, the M in the theory's name could stand for "magic," or "mystery" and the true meaning should be decided once a more fundamental formulation of the theory is known. Although there is underlying mathematical theory to support M-brane, it is too complex for a layperson to understand. Outside of academic circles, M-brane theory is discussed conceptually, as an idea accepted in good faith. Currently, no experimental evidence exists to verify that M-brane theory is an accurate description of the real world.[11]

Cohle explains his interpretation of M-brane theory by asking the detectives to imagine an impossible vantage point, a perspective outside everything that exists in the physical world. From that impossible standpoint, one would see time as "a flat circle," a single structure comprised of every moment of every life that ever existed, every possible future and past

---

[9] *True Detective*. "Seeing Things." Episode 2. Directed by Cary Joji Fukunaga. Written by Nic Pizzolatto. HBO. January 19, 2014.

[10] M-Brane is a theory in physics which could lead to a unified theory of all the fundamental forces in nature (e.g. gravitational, electromagnetic). Scientists of all stripes will likely take issue with M-brane theory being placed in the same class of unseen worlds with the Kingdom of God and the lost city of Carcosa. The religious and fictional unseen worlds have no scientific research to support their existence. M-brane theory, while not complete, does have the basic mathematical structure established and the structure is in agreement with other string theories.

[11] Jones, Andrew Zimmerman and Daniel Robbins. *String Theory for Dummies*. Indianapolis: Wiley Publishing, 2010.

compressed into a single shape. "See, everything outside our dimension," Cohle informs the detectives, "that's eternity looking down on us." In his attempt to explain a scientific theory, Cohle ends up describing the viewpoint of an omnipotent god looking down at all of creation. As a layman, Cohle lacks the scientific expertise necessary to test or prove the existence of the eternal vantage point he describes. It exists for him because he believes in it, just as Joel Theriot believes in the Kingdom of God and Reggie Ledoux believes in Carcosa. Cohle's looking to the sky and imagining "eternity looking down on us,"[12] echoes of Theriot and Ledoux looking to the heavens and declaring "he sees you."

Like the parishioners at the Friends of Christ tent revival, Cohle is a desperate man. He is haunted by the death of his young daughter and no amount of drinking, drugs, or violence can numb his pain for long. Although he disparages the idea of closure, this is exactly what his M-brane inspired ideology gives him. The belief that all time exists simultaneously and that no one moment is more significant than another renders life a meaningless repetition of patterns. It allows Cohle to devalue experiences in the physical world in the same way that Joel Theriot encourages Christians to view their "angers and griefs and separations" as nothing more than a "fevered hallucination."[13] However, where Christianity and the Yellow King cult offer their believers hope with the promise of a life after death in a spiritual realm, Cohle's ideology presents death as its own reward or release. For him, an eternity of non-existence in the void is preferable to the pain and toil of life. This is the logic which allows him to reframe his daughter's untimely death as something other than a tragedy. As he admits to Detectives Gilbough and Papina, Cohle sometimes feels grateful that his daughter was spared the pointless, repetitive grind of life in the physical world. "Isn't that a beautiful way to go out," he asks, "painlessly as a happy child?"[14]

---

[12] *True Detective.* "Who Goes There." Episode 4. Directed by Cary Joji Fukunaga. Written by Nic Pizzolatto. HBO. February 9, 2014.
[13] *True Detective.* "The Locked Room." Episode 3. Directed by Cary Joji Fukunaga. Written by Nic Pizzolatto. HBO. January 26, 2014.
[14] *True Detective.* "Seeing Things." Episode 2. Directed by Cary Joji Fukunaga. Written by Nic Pizzolatto. HBO. January 19, 2014.

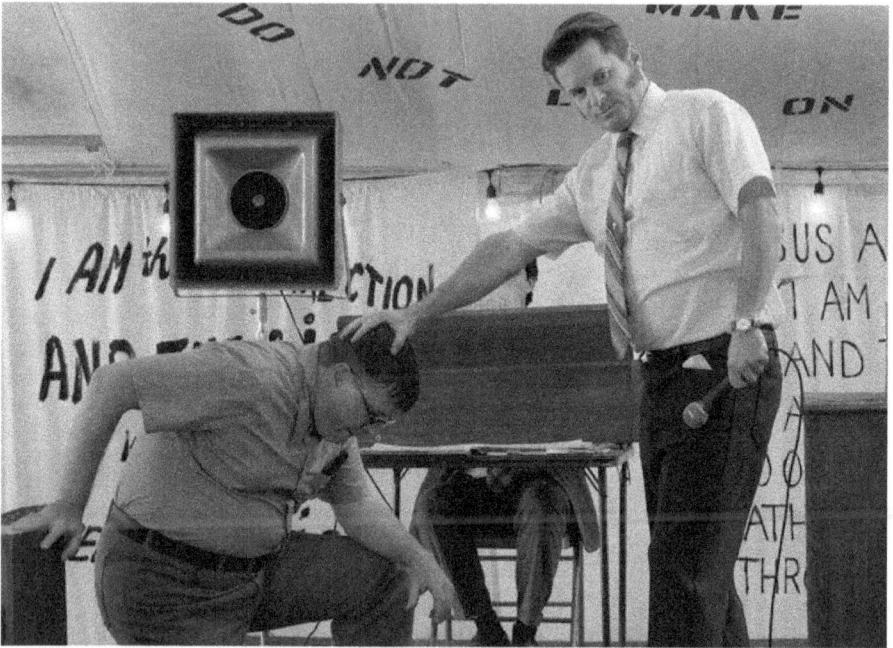

Tent revival preacher Joel Theriot ministers to his downtrodden flock. *True Detective*, season 1, episode 3, "The Locked Room." HBO.

> Come die with me, little priest.
> — Errol Childress

Cohle's disdain for religion does not prevent him from appropriating a Christian symbol as the focal point of his meditations on the nature of reality. A crucifix hangs on the wall of his Spartan apartment, the lone adornment on a bare white wall. When Hart asks about it, Cohle provides an explanation that focuses on the crucifix as a representation of a willing acceptance of death. "It's a form of meditation," he tells Hart. "I contemplate the moment in the garden, the idea of allowing your own crucifixion."[15] For Cohle, meditating on the crucifix creates a new significance for death. Building on the Christian narrative of Christ's death as an atonement for the sins of all human kind, the crucifix becomes a symbol of meaningful sacrifice, of choosing personal suffering to advance a greater good. Cohle's meditation on the symbol signals his desire to change his personal narrative through an act of self-sacrifice. He seeks to rewrite the ugly reality that his life has been a "circle of violence and

---

[15] *True Detective*. "The Long Bright Dark." Episode 1. Directed by Cary Joji Fukunaga. Written by Nic Pizzolatto. HBO. January 12, 2014.

degradation,"[16] and recast himself as a heroic martyr, one who suffers for the benefit of others.

Depiction of Christ on the cross emphasizing his crown of thorns. Image courtesy of Pexels.com.

Crucifixion imagery appears in the earliest scenes of *True Detective* as Hart and Cohle first examine Dora Lange's body.[17] Cohle refers to the crime scene as "ritual... iconography,"[18] an observation which encourages the audience to draw parallels between the victim's body and that of established religious icons. Like Jesus on the cross, Dora's body is stripped nude and publicly displayed. Her hands are tied, binding her to the trunk of an oak tree, similar to how Jesus is portrayed as bound hand and foot to a wooden cross. Dora's corpse bears the marks of the cruelty she was subjected to before her death, notably the stab

---

[16] *True Detective*. "After You've Gone." Episode 7. Directed by Cary Joji Fukunaga. Written by Nic Pizzolatto. HBO. March 2, 2014.

[17] Crucifixion imagery is also present in the 2012 Lake Charles murder photos which Detectives Gilbough and Papina show to Cohle in S1:E7. In the Lake Charles case the victim is suspended from a bridge by multiple ropes, posing her naked body with arms outstretched, head down and feet dangling, much like Jesus on the cross. Like Dora Lange, the Lake Charles victim is found with a crown of horns on her head.

[18] *True Detective*. "The Long Bright Dark." Episode 1. Directed by Cary Joji Fukunaga. Written by Nic Pizzolatto. HBO. January 12, 2014.

wound on her left side, which evokes the damage caused when one of the Roman soldiers "with a spear pierced His [Jesus's] side"[19] at the crucifixion.

Another important similarity between the staging of Dora Lange's corpse and the crucifixion of Jesus is the fact that they both wear crowns. As part of their abuse of Jesus, Roman soldiers twisted together a crown of thorns and placed it upon his head, making a mockery of his role as "king of the Jews."[20] Though the crown of thorns was no doubt painful, it is symbolic of suffering that is beyond physical pain. The crown, originally a symbol of majesty and nobility, becomes a tool of ridicule, mocking Jesus for his selfless sacrifice and his hope for the redemption of all mankind.

The crown of horns[21] and branches on Dora Lange's head are another point of connection between the symbolism of Christianity and the Yellow King cult. When viewed through the lens of Christian imagery, Dora's crown is symbolic of humiliation and self-sacrifice. The key difference between her crown and the crown of Christ is the addition of antlers to Dora's crown. Horns, especially when worn on the head, are associated with animalistic sexuality, as illustrated by the mythological creatures of the satyr and the Minotaur. When coupled with the Christian imagery present in the rest of the scene, the horns on Dora's crown become a clue that the humiliation Dora suffered before her death was sexual. As a prostitute, Dora was no stranger to being scorned by society, ridiculed for being so desperate that she would sell her body just to survive. Like Christ, Dora suffered physically and emotionally, experiencing the gamut of human pain before her sacrificial death.

The crucifixion imagery used to stage Dora Lange's body and her familiarity with the life after death promised by Christianity supports the theory that Dora may have been a willing sacrifice to the Yellow King. Her Christian faith indoctrinated her to the idea that suffering and self-sacrifice are virtuous.

---

[19] John 19:34. In *Holy Bible: NRSV, New Revised Standard Version*. New York: Harper Bibles, 2007.

[20] Matthew 27:29. In *Holy Bible: NRSV, New Revised Standard Version*. New York: Harper Bibles, 2007.

[21] The image of a stag burdened by an over-heavy rack of antlers or horns is a central image to Peter Wessel Zapffe's classic essay, "The Last Messiah." For more on the connection between Zapffe's philosophy, and Dora Lange's crown of horns, see chapter 8, "Compensating for a Tragic Misstep in Evolution: Zapffe's Strategies for Minimizing Consciousness."

Weakening her ability to think critically, Christianity also encouraged her to look for her reward in the Kingdom of God rather than in this life. If Dora was introduced to the idea of sacrificing herself to the Yellow King as a form of martyrdom or salvation, it might not have seemed strange to her. Christianity taught Dora that death isn't just the end of life, it is a transformative event, the only way to break through the veil between the physical world and the unseen world of heaven. Like Rust Cohle, Dora had an ideological framework in place that allowed her to embrace self-sacrifice as a way to escape the pain of this life for the promise of an alternate reality.

> Your sorrows pin you to this place.
> — Joel Theriot

Pizzolatto's portrayal of religion as a method of manipulating reality could be seen as disparaging to believers, but a closer look at Rust Cohle's belief system offers a counterpoint to that assessment. Cohle is a staunch atheist and looks down on the faithful gathered at the Friends of Christ tent revival, but is blind to how much he has in common with them. Like the simple folks gathered to hear a message of hope, Cohle has experienced sorrow and suffering. The death of his daughter, the dissolution of his marriage, and years of addiction make him susceptible to the allure of an unseen world. Too cynical for religion, Cohle believes in the "flat circle" view of the universe. The description of Cohle's unseen universe comes from theoretical physics instead of a holy book, but it amounts to belief in a world other than the physical space he inhabits every day. By comparing Christianity, the Yellow King cult, and Cohle's secular belief in a version of an unseen world, Pizzolatto suggests that belief in an alternate reality or unseen worlds does not indicate a weakness of spirit or mind unique to religious individuals. Rather, when faced with deep pain and suffering, people re-shape the narrative of their lives using religion. It is one of the many stories we tell ourselves, a narrative framework that provides solace in the idea that there are better worlds than the reality we face every day.

A Giant Gutter in Outer Space: Cosmic Insignificance in *True Detective* and "The Dunwich Horror"

Cosmic horror is commonly associated with eldritch abominations, mad gods, inconceivable terrors, and the works of H.P. Lovecraft. Though he did not invent cosmic horror, Lovecraft was able to neatly summarize the spirit of the genre. He explained that, "...all my tales are based on the fundamental premise that common human laws and interests and emotions have no validity or significance in the vast cosmos-at-large."[1] Cosmic horror stems from the terrible realization that we live in a cold, uncaring, unreasonable universe and that there is nothing we can do to protect ourselves from it. This is a terrifying, but abstract idea that can be difficult to use as a basis for narrative conflict. Lovecraft's approach to this problem was to create a loose pantheon of gods and monsters to represent the vastness of the universe and powers beyond human comprehension. After Lovecraft's death, other authors built on his ideas, turning them into the larger Cthulu mythos, which has lived on in fiction, film, and games. However, as chilling as entities like Cthulu and Nyarlathotep

---

[1] 1927 letter to Farnsworth Wright.

may be, they are representations of existential terror in cosmic horror, not the defining elements of the genre. One of Lovecraft's stories, "The Dunwich Horror,"[2] and *True Detective* illustrate this point. Both stories use supernatural elements, but also rely on the uncanny and existential dread to convey the horror of humanity's insignificance in the cosmos.

> I don't like this place. Nothing grows in the right direction.
> — Rust Cohle

True Detective starts from the ground up in setting the mood for cosmic horror. The twisting swamps and bayous of Southern Louisiana are perfect visuals for the alien geometries which permeate Lovecraft's fiction. Cypress trees rise from murky water like eldritch creatures, draped in tattered capes of moss and vine. At the outset of the narrative, Detective Cohle is new to the area and immediately feels the strangeness of the bayou in a way that other characters do not. Cohle attempts to describe the feeling. "This place is like somebody's memory of a town, and the memory is fading. It's like there was never anything here but jungle."[3] Cohle's line recalls the beginning of Lovecraft's "The Dunwich Horror." In it, the narrator of the tale, Doctor Armitage, describes the area around the town as beautiful, teeming with tall trees, wild grasses carpeting gently sloping hills. Yet at the same time, he notes that the environment gives a feeling of being "somehow confronted with hidden things."[4]

Cohle's idea that there is something inherently unnatural about Vermilion Parish is an example of uncanny atmosphere, a trope H.P. Lovecraft often used in his fiction. The uncanny is a psychological experience, a feeling that there is an illusion at work, or some other reality lurking beneath what can be seen. It is

---

[2] It's worth noting that "The Dunwich Horror" is an atypical Lovecraft story in that it has a "happy" ending where humanity prevails over alien gods (albeit temporarily). It can be viewed as a pastiche of the works of influential fantasy and horror author Arthur Machen. Lovecraft scholars point to similarities between "The Dunwich Horror" and Machen's novella "The Great God Plan" (1894) as well as his short story "The White People" (1904).

[3] *True Detective*. "The Long Bright Dark." Episode 1. Directed by Cary Joji Fukunaga. Written by Nic Pizzolatto. HBO. January 12, 2014.

[4] Lovecraft, H. P. "The Dunwich Horror." *Tales of the Cthulhu Mythos*. New York: Del Rey, 1998.

an eerie feeling, "something that should have remained hidden … has come into the open."[5] Note that although the "hidden" element is often supernatural, mundane environments can be uncanny as well. In *True Detective*, Cohle makes his observation while looking at an empty parking lot. This patch of asphalt holds no supernatural or occult significance to the larger narrative, but it still seems *wrong* in a way that he can't quite explain.

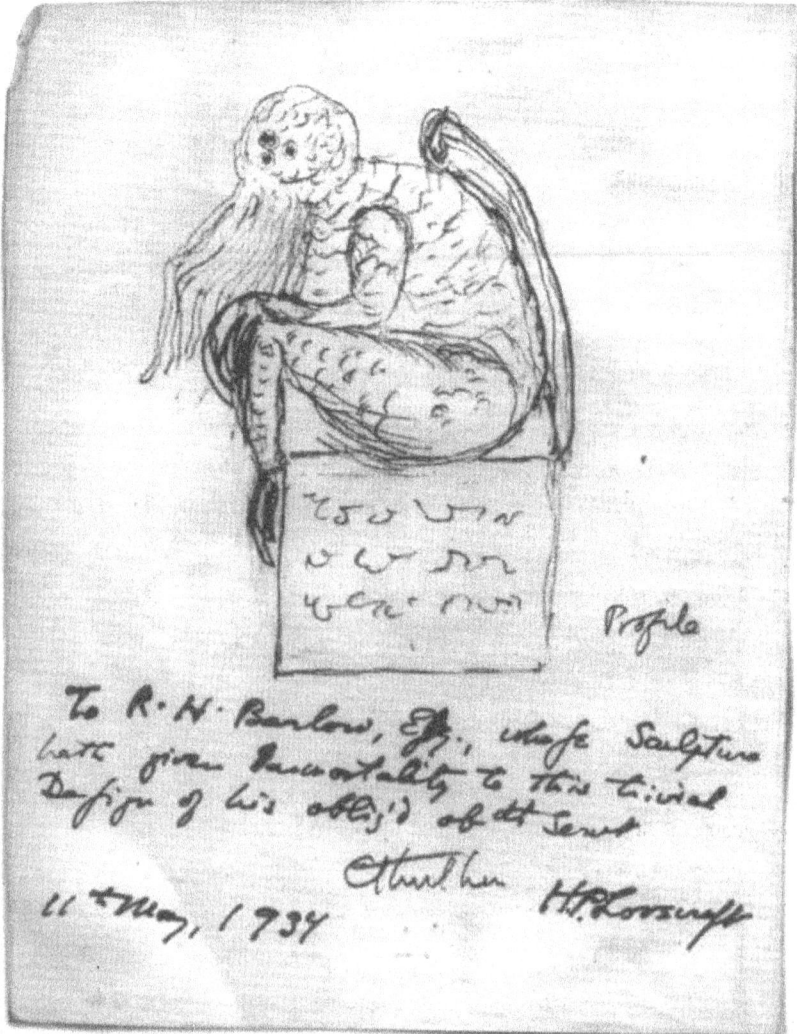

1934 sketch by H.P. Lovecraft depicting a statuette of Cthulu.

---

[5] Friedrich Wilhelm Joseph von Schelling, as cited by Freud in "The Uncanny," *The Uncanny*, translated by David McLintock, New York, Penguin, 2003, p. 148.

Both Lovecraft and Pizzolatto use uncanny atmosphere early in their stories to establish a quiet sense of unease before the real tension of the narrative begins to build. It's also a subtle way to foreshadow the idea of a powerful inhuman force invading human space. Humanity operates within the natural world. We may live in houses and drive in cars, but we still live at the whims of nature - earthquakes, storms, droughts, invasive species, bacterial blooms — these events are completely natural and real threats to the existence of humanity. In *True Detective*, Hart and Cohle's investigation is hampered by records lost to hurricanes and flooding. In "The Dunwich Horror," plant life overgrows houses and roads, completely indifferent to human life and endeavors. In both stories, the natural world is a powerful entity with no interest in human life, although it is an entity so familiar as to go unnoticed by most people. Cosmic horror, however, is really about something much, much bigger than what happens on a tiny speck like the planet Earth.

> ...the terrible and secret fate of all life.
> — Rust Cohle

Secret truths and forbidden knowledge abound in cosmic horror, but it all boils down to the same thing: humanity is insignificant and helpless against inhuman powers "beyond all spheres of force and matter, space and time."[6] This truth can be revealed in the narrative through a variety of mechanisms.

Lovecraft buries mind-shattering truths within ancient books. He created the *Necronomicon*,[7] a fictional grimoire which describes cosmic forces beyond

---

[6] Lovecraft, H. P. "The Dunwich Horror." *Tales of the Cthulhu Mythos*. New York: Del Rey, 1998.

[7] Lovecraft never specified the exact contents of the *Necronomicon*, which made it easy for other horror authors, artists, and directors to cite it in their own fictional works. The *Necronomicon* has taken on a life of its own, as some fans believe that the book is real. During his lifetime Lovecraft received several letters asking about the book's authenticity and libraries still receive requests for the book today. The line between fantasy and reality was further muddied in the late 1970's when a book came out claiming to be a translation of the "true" *Necronomicon*. The book had very little to do with the Lovecraft mythos and was mostly based on Sumerian mythology. The introduction was written under the pseudonym "Simon," which is why some Lovecraft fans refer to the book as the "Simonomicon." This publication opened the door for a flood of other interpretations and imaginings, each one claiming to be the "true" *Necronomicon*. Like Shub-Niggurath, The Black Goat of the

human understanding and details the existence of Elder Gods and Great Old Ones like Cthulu. The *Necronomicon* appears in several of Lovecraft's stories, including "The Dunwich Horror." In this tale, Lovecraft emphasizes that the *Necronomicon* and the knowledge it contains are so dangerous that it must be kept under lock and key at the Miskatonic University library. When Dr. Armitage, the head librarian of Miskatonic University, is tasked with deciphering notes taken from the *Necronomicon,* he finds a truth too nightmarish to be comprehended. This information shatters Dr. Armitage's hold on reality, weakening him physically and mentally. Dr. Armitage subsequently falls into a delirium in which he raves about "elder things" threatening to strip the earth bare and "drag it away from the... cosmos of matter into some other plane."[8]

In Lovecraft's stories, the true nature of the universe is incompatible with humanity's understanding of the world, because humanity's reality is based on an illusion of order and safety. In the human perception of reality, Earth occupies a fixed position in space. People can rely on this fact and don't need to fear being dragged into an alternate plane of existence by vastly powerful beings. Reading from the *Necronomicon* pulled aside the veil for Dr. Armitage, revealing the terrifying truth that his perception of reality was woefully inaccurate.

> What happened to my head, it's not something that gets better.
> — Rust Cohle

In *True Detective*, the secret truth of the universe isn't revealed in an ancient book. Cohle discovers it through personal experience, namely the death of his daughter. At the outset of *True Detective* Cohle is disillusioned, but before the events of the narrative, Cohle was a family man. Marrying and having a child indicate that Cohle bought into the illusion that there was order to the universe. He believed he had control over his life and that he could protect the people he loved. With the death of his daughter, that illusion was shattered. As an older man, Cohle understands "the hubris it must take to yank a soul out of

---

Woods with a Thousand Young, Lovecraft's *Necronomicon* is mother to a chaotic horde of titles which grows larger every day.

[8] Lovecraft, H. P. "The Dunwich Horror." *Tales of the Cthulhu Mythos*. New York: Del Rey, 1998.

nonexistence, into this meat... to force life into this thresher."[9] Cohle's view of life is so bleak that he claims to be glad his daughter died young, as it meant she was spared the cruelties of a cold and chaotic world.

Cohle's experience after learning the horror of human insignificance mirrors Dr. Armitage's collapse in "The Dunwich Horror." He did not immediately succumb to madness, but Cohle did suffer a mental breakdown after adopting a violent, drug-fueled, nihilistic persona for his undercover police work. Cohle's hallucinations and synesthesia are the side effects of trying to reconcile two incompatible realities – the pleasant illusion of everyday life and the horrible truth of the universe. The symptoms Cohle suffers are also another example of the uncanny in *True Detective*. "Feelings of uncertainty, in particular regarding the reality of who one is and what is being experienced,"[10] are a hallmark of the uncanny. They are also core to Cohle's struggles to maintain a grasp on reality. In his interview with Gilbough and Papina, Cohle describes how it feels to distrust his own perceptions. "Most of the time I was convinced I'd lost it," he explains to the younger detectives, "but there were other times I thought I was mainlining the secret truth of the universe."[11]

It should be noted that Cohle's reality-shattering event is in no way supernatural. Despite humanity's best attempts to preserve life, children die every day in tragic accidents and from illnesses for which there is no cure. Most people get through the day by ignoring this horrific truth and telling themselves that if they do all the right things they will be safe, that chaos and entropy can be prevented through human action. People like Cohle and Dr. Armitage, however, have seen the true insignificance and helplessness of mankind and find no comfort in illusions.

> My family's been here a long, long time.
> — Errol Childress

Characters in cosmic horror do not all react in the same way upon encountering the horrible truth of the cosmos. Rather than being driven mad by

---

[9] *True Detective*. "Seeing Things." Episode 2. Directed by Cary Joji Fukunaga. Written by Nic Pizzolatto. HBO. January 19, 2014.
[10] Royle, Nicholas. The Uncanny. Manchester: Manchester University Press, 2008.
[11] *True Detective*. "Seeing Things." Episode 2. Directed by Cary Joji Fukunaga. Written by Nic Pizzolatto. HBO. January 19, 2014.

learning this secret truth, these characters are corrupted by it. They stare into the void, losing themselves to the vast nothingness, and becoming vessels for ancient gods.

Lovecraft's fiction draws on the Southern gothic trope of dynastic families that have split into a wholesome branch and a corrupted branch. In "The Dunwich Horror," the bifurcated family is the Whatleys and the focus is on Wilbur Whately, an illegitimate son of the corrupted branch of the family. This degenerate group performs "unhallowed rites... wild orgiastic prayers" at the stone ruins atop the rolling Dunwich hills, calling forth "forbidden shapes of shadow."[12] *True Detective* features a similar dynamic with Errol Childress as the illegitimate son of the upstanding Tuttle family. Like Whatley, Childress engages in occult worship in a remote location, calling out to a mysterious deity called the Yellow King.

Errol Childress, a physical embodiment of existential terror. *True Detective*, season 1, episode 8, "Form and Void." HBO.

Wilbur Whateley and Errol Childress are lesser members of their illustrious families, aware of both the greatness in their bloodline and their own tangential relationship to that power. Ostracized by their families and society, Whately and Childress are not repelled by the idea of cosmic insignificance. For them,

---

[12] Lovecraft, H. P. "The Dunwich Horror." *Tales of the Cthulhu Mythos*. New York: Del Rey, 1998.

the prospect of complete erasure of the self is an escape from their lowly position in society. Worshipping inhuman deities allows the men to embrace an alien indifference to all human order, laws, and values. Released from the rules of human morality, Whately and Childress become monsters - physical embodiments of an existential terror. They have rejected their humanity and in doing so, have become alien rather than alienated.

> Death is not the end.
> — Miss Delores

In fiction, the death of a monster often signals the end of the story. It's a familiar pattern of conflict and resolution, of order ruling over chaos, but in cosmic horror death offers no closure. The protagonists of True Detective and "The Dunwich Horror" succeed in killing their monstrous antagonists. However, these deaths are temporary victories for humanity. Wilbur Whately and Errol Childress are only worshippers of a vast, inhuman power. Killing them prevents these powers from gaining greater access to Earth, but it does nothing to change the fundamental nature of the universe or to elevate humanity's place within it.

Lovecraft ends "The Dunwich Horror" with an assurance that the townsfolk will "pull down the rings and the standing stones on the other hills"[13] to prevent other cultists from using them as a place to commune with the elder gods. Similarly, at the close of True Detective, Hart and Cohle attempt to expose the misdeeds of the Tuttle family in an effort to limit their occult worship. In both stories the actions seem like an insufficient defense against further evil, but in True Detective the futility is made explicit. Detectives Hart and Cohle succeed in stopping Errol Childress, but they fail to connect his actions to the perversity of the powerful Tuttle family. The evening news rolls footage of bodies being exhumed at the Childress home while the newscaster reports "the state Attorney General and the F.B.I. have discredited rumors that the accused was in some way related to Louisiana Senator, Edwin Tuttle."[14]

In the end, the occult and supernatural elements associated with Wilbur Whately and Errol Childress are not the most disturbing aspects of "The

---

[13] Ibid.
[14] True Detective. "After You've Gone." Episode 7. Directed by Cary Joji Fukunaga. Written by Nic Pizzolatto. HBO. March 2, 2014.

Dunwich Horror" and *True Detective*. The lasting impact stems from Dr. Armitage and Cohle electing to preserve the illusion that human life has any significance in the larger cosmos, even though they have seen beyond veil to the horrors of the cosmos. They prop up a pleasant lie about reality, because that is the most they can do to shelter humanity from a vast, uncaring universe.

All the King's Children are Marked: Signs of the King in Yellow in *True Detective*

Robert W. Chambers's 1894 collection of short stories *The King in Yellow*[1] is an influential work of weird fiction that is "ripe with derangement, haunting beauty and eerie torments."[2] Part of the mystique of Chambers's creation is that it is three distinct things all at once: a collection of short stories, a fictional play which appears in the collection of short stories,[3] and a supernatural entity

---

[1] *The King in Yellow* is in the public domain. eBook files are available to download for free at via the Gutenberg project. http://www.gutenberg.org/ebooks/8492.

[2] Steele, Justin, and Joseph S. Pulver. "Interview: Joe Pulver Talks the King in Yellow." The Arkham Digest. March 02, 2014. Accessed October 02, 2018. http://www.arkhamdigest.com/2014/03/interview-joe-pulver-talks-king-in.html. Joseph S. Pulver is a renowned Yellow Mythos author and editor. In an interview with The Arkham Digest he details how the original Chambers's King in Yellow has been expanded and merged with H.P. Lovecraft's Cthulu mythos by other authors, editors, and gaming enthusiasts. For the purposes of this essay, the author refers to only the original stories written by Chambers.

[3] Though the book contains several stories, only the first four entries relate to the King in Yellow. They are "The Repairer of Reputations," "The Mask," "The Court of the Yellow Dragon," and "The Yellow Sign." Taken collectively, they form what fans

appearing in both the play and the book. Chambers quotes only a few lines of the play in his stories, hinting that anyone who reads the second act of the play will be driven insane by the revelation of horrific truths about the universe that no human mind could possibly comprehend. The lines of the play which appear in the stories are from the darkly poetic first act, which lures unsuspecting readers closer to the King in Yellow. The character of the King in Yellow is the lord of an unseen world. The King in Yellow's supernatural realm is removed from our reality, but threatens to break through to the earthly plane of existence. Loosely human in form, the cryptic King in Yellow is identified by his tattered robes and his Yellow Sign. As the book's name suggests, it is the inspiration for many of the occult and cosmic horror elements in *True Detective*.

Given that *The King in Yellow* has a rich and firmly established mythos, it is easy to find signs of its influence everywhere in *True Detective*. One of the most popular fan theories is that that there is a "Yellow King" in *True Detective*, a character analogous to the supernatural King in Yellow from Chamber's fiction. However, the search for a singular, villainous Yellow King isn't in keeping with the dreamlike fluidity of Chambers's original work or how it informs the cosmic horror elements in *True Detective*. The influence of *The King in Yellow* is more diffuse and permeates the world of *True Detective* through the Yellow Sign, the lure of Carcosa, and the motif of masks and unmasking.

> Reggie's got this brand on his back, like a spiral. He says that's their sign.
> — Charlie Lange

The Yellow Sign is a symbol which appears in several stories in *The King in Yellow*. Much like other elements of the yellow mythos, the exact shape of the Yellow Sign is never clearly defined.[4] In a short story of the same name, Chambers describes the Yellow Sign is described as "a curious symbol or letter in gold. It was neither Arabic or Chinese, nor... did it belong to any human

---

refer to as the "Yellow Mythos" – a set of characters, settings, symbols and motifs associated with the King in Yellow.

[4] Several artists have tried to recreate the Yellow Sign, but the most well-known interpretation is the 1989 glyph designed by Kevin Ross for the Call of Cthulu role playing game. The version of the design which appeared in print was actually a corruption of the original design, as it was printed both upside down and backwards. It seems the Yellow Sign is determined to remain enigmatic.

The 1895 printing of *The King in Yellow* with cover design by the author, Robert W. Chambers.

script."[5] Anyone who gazes upon the sign risks descending into madness and opens themselves to the influence of The King in Yellow. It acts as the seal of the King, foretelling his appearance and marking his acolytes and sacrifices.

In *True Detective*, the spiral functions much like the Yellow Sign in Chambers's work. The spiral first appears on Dora Lange's body and alerts Cohle that there is an occultic or ritualistic nature to her murder. A later interview with Charlie Lange, Dora's estranged husband, confirms that the spiral is the sign of the Yellow King cult. The connection Charlie makes between the spiral and stories of cult sacrifice is supported by entries in Dora's diary. She wrote, "The King's children are marked. They became his angels."[6] The spiral on Dora's back marks her as a cult sacrifice, just as the spirals on Reggie Ledoux and Errol Childress mark them as cult members.

In Chambers's works artists, and other creative types are particularly susceptible to the mind-clouding power of the Yellow Sign. In the short story "The Yellow Sign," a painter and his model encounter the sign on a piece of onyx jewelry and soon find themselves suffering horrific dreams, hallucinations, and lost time.

Rust Cohle is not an artist *per se*, but he is creatively inclined. His notebook is filled with detailed sketches of Dora Lange's body, spirals, crowns of horns, and the complicated twig sculptures found at the crime scene. In 2012, when he reconnects with Marty Hart, Cohle muses on other careers he could have pursued. "I suppose I could have been a painter, a historian. Old scenes, new details."[7] Cohle's artistic bent makes him vulnerable to the corrupting influence of the spiral, *True Detective*'s version of The Yellow Sign. Cohle admits to suffering hallucinations before arriving in Louisiana and taking on the Dora Lange murder case, but after he sees the spiral Cohle's hallucinations take on a spiral theme. These visions take place when Cohle is at locations associated with the cult, as is the case when the detectives visit the burned-out church and

---

[5] Chambers, Robert W. *The King in Yellow*. New York, NY: Fall River Press, 2014. Contains the full text of Robert W. Chambers's stories as well as an introduction and notes by S. T. Joshi. Originally published 1895.

[6] *True Detective*. "Seeing Things." Episode 2. Directed by Cary Joji Fukunaga. Written by Nic Pizzolatto. HBO. January 19, 2014.

[7] *True Detective*. "After You've Gone." Episode 7. Directed by Cary Joji Fukunaga. Written by Nic Pizzolatto. HBO. March 2, 2014.

Cohle sees a flock of birds form a spiral pattern, flying with seemingly unnatural precision.

Much like the Yellow Sign in Chambers's work, the spiral in *True Detective* triggers paranoia and self-doubt in characters who see it, even for a character as skeptical as Cohle. The spiral on Dora's body and the spirals which appear at locations connected with the investigation are physical evidence of *something*, but much of the other evidence is so weird that it is difficult for Cohle to separate reality from prison gossip, or the fantastical imaginings of cult members. Each new lead Cohle finds introduces another implausible angle to the case. Under these circumstances, even the most analytical person could begin to doubt his grasp on reality. Additionally, the idea that Cohle may be marked in a way that he cannot see or feel creates a sense of helplessness and alienation from the self. He suffers a unique terror in feeling that that there is some unknown, malevolent agent hidden within his own mind. As the Dora Lange investigation wears on, Cohle admits to "pulling lost time,"[8] leaving him with uncertainty about what he was doing during those blackout periods.

By the time Cohle confronts Errol Childress in the overgrown tunnels of Carcosa,[9] the spiral is so much a part of him that he may as well have it branded on his body like Reggie Ledoux or Dora Lange. The spiral has marked Cohle and lured him ever closer to the Yellow King. It is in Carcosa that Cohle encounters the final and most dangerous version of the spiral. At a key moment in his hunt for Errol Childress, Cohle hallucinates a massive spiral galaxy floating a just a few feet above his head. This image harkens back to Chambers's idea of Carcosa as an alternate dimension, something as wholly unnatural and unfathomable by the human mind. It also marks Cohle as a sacrifice, for as he stands transfixed by the spiral galaxy, Errol Childress rushes in to stab him. Just as the characters in Chambers's fiction follow the Yellow Sign to their doom, Cohle follows the spiral and nearly dies in Carcosa, in front of the Yellow King's altar and staring at

---

[8] *True Detective*. "Haunted Houses." Episode 6. Directed by Cary Joji Fukunaga. Written by Nic Pizzolatto. HBO. February 23, 2014.

[9] The location used to shoot the Carcosa scenes is Fort Macomb, a 19th century military installation that once guarded New Orleans. Originally named Fort Chef Menteur, and later named Fort Wood, it saw limited action in the Civil War. Decommissioned in 1871, the fort has been nearly forgotten and left to crumble. Fort Macomb is unsafe for visitors, but nearby Fort Pike was built to the same design and is open to the public.

the spiral sigil of the Yellow King.

> Black stars rise... You're in Carcosa now.
> — Reggie Ledoux

The idea of a lost city named Carcosa does not originate with Robert Chambers. Carcosa first appears in an 1891 short story by Ambrose Bierce, "An Inhabitant of Carcosa." The Bierce story does not provide much by way of a description of the city, but it struck a chord with Chambers, who elaborated on the idea in his own fiction. The lost city of Carcosa appears repeatedly in *The King in Yellow*. In Chambers's work the city is a cursed place with a landscape which suggests that it exists on another planet or floating somewhere in space. It is the domain over which The King in Yellow rules. The most detailed description of the city appears in the play version of The King in Yellow in "Cassilda's Song":

> Along the shore the cloud waves break,
> The twin suns sink behind the lake,
> The shadows lengthen
> In Carcosa.
>
> Strange is the night where black stars rise,
> And strange moons circle through the skies,
> But stranger still is
> Lost Carcosa.[10]

In *True Detective*, it's unclear if Carcosa is a physical location, a spiritual/psychological state of being, or perhaps both at once. The first mention of it comes from Dora's estranged husband, Charlie Lange. Recounting his experience sharing a prison cell with Reggie Ledoux, Charlie tells the detectives "He said that, they... sacrifice kids ... something about someplace called Carcosa and the Yellow King. He said there's all these, like, old stones out in the woods, people go to, like, worship."[11] Charlie's information points to Carcosa being a location on Earth, possibly the crumbling tunnels where Errol Childress keeps his shrine to the Yellow King. However, the Carcosa Dora Lange describes in her diary doesn't match with Charlie's account or the labyrinthine structure Errol

---

[10] Chambers, Robert W. *The King in Yellow*. New York, NY: Fall River Press, 2014.
[11] *True Detective*. "Who Goes There." Episode 4. Directed by Cary Joji Fukunaga. Written by Nic Pizzolatto. HBO. February 9, 2014.

Childress haunts. On a page opposite the scrawled name "The Yellow King" Dora copied "Cassilda's Song" in her diary – the two stanzas quoted above. Doodles of black stars and two crescent moons flank the lines, echoing the imagery of Chambers's otherworldly depiction. The physical reality of Carcosa is called into question again when the detectives capture Reggie Ledoux outside his squalid compound. Ledoux tells Cohle, "you're in Carcosa now."[12] Since the Ledoux compound doesn't appear to have the old stones from Charlie's description or the twin suns and cloud waves of Dora's description, the Carcosa Reggie mentions must be something other than his physical location. Looking up at the bright blue sky, he claims to see the black stars rising, supporting the idea that Carcosa exists in his mind or in some other reality.

Much like the Yellow Symbol, Carcosa functions as another lure into madness and death. Carcosa is a lost city that cannot be found, defined, or mapped. Contemplating Carcosa addles the brain because the human mind is not built to see a city that is here and not here at the same time. In *True Detective*, as in Chambers's work, the only way to see Carcosa is to submit to the Yellow King. Once gifted with secret knowledge of Carcosa, members of the Yellow King cult are drawn to it and to death, as Reggie Ledoux demonstrates when he is captured by the detectives. Reggie is unsurprised to face death, asking Cohle, "It's time, isn't it?"[13] Rather than fear for his life, Ledoux calmly awaits the bullet that will end his life and allow him to join the Yellow King in the lost city. For Yellow King cult members, Earth is just a stage. If an acolyte makes the right sacrifices and performs all the required rituals, he can escape the mortal "disc in the loop."[14]

The appearance of an exact quote describing Carcosa, as it appears in "Cassilda's Song," highlights the manufactured nature of the narrative in *True Detective* and introduces a metafictional element to the Yellow King cult. In one of the first scenes of the show, Cohle concludes that her killer is a "meta-

---

[12] *True Detective*. "Form and Void." Episode 8. Directed by Cary Joji Fukunaga. Written by Nic Pizzolatto. HBO. March 9, 2014.

[13] *True Detective*. "The Secret Fate of All Life." Episode 5. Directed by Cary Joji Fukunaga. Written by Nic Pizzolatto. HBO. February 16, 2014.

[14] *True Detective*. "Form and Void." Episode 8. Directed by Cary Joji Fukunaga. Written by Nic Pizzolatto. HBO. March 9, 2014.

psychotic,"[15] and that the murder is more than random violence. "It's fantasy reenactment," he explains to Hart, "ritual... fetishization... iconography."[16] For Cohle, the spiral and crown on Dora Lange's body are evidence of a performance, props that Errol Childress uses to act out a narrative of his own creation.[17] This makes Childress an author of sorts, staging his own live-action interpretation of *The King in Yellow* play, featuring all the symbolism of the Carcosa and the Yellow Mythos.

Reggie Ledoux prepares to ascend beyond the disc in the loop. *True Detective*, season 1, episode 5, "The Secret Fate of All Life." HBO.

When Cohle comes in contact with cult members Dewall and Reggie Ledoux, they both act as if they know something about Cohle that he does not know about himself. While being held at gunpoint, Reggie Ledoux babbles about black stars rising before fixing his eyes on Cohle and declaring, "I know

---

[15] *True Detective*. "The Long Bright Dark." Episode 1. Directed by Cary Joji Fukunaga. Written by Nic Pizzolatto. HBO. January 12, 2014.
[16] Ibid.
[17] Note another metafictional detail in Episode 8, "Form and Void." As Errol Childress enters his squalid home a scene from *North by Northwest* (Hitchcock, 1959) plays on a television in the parlor. It's no accident that the film is about mistaken identities and assumed identities. Childress pauses, entranced as Cary Grant declares, "With such expert playacting, you make this very room a theater."

what happens next. I saw you in my dream... You'll do this again."[18] Reggie's prophecy suggests that there is something shared between Reggie and Cohle, a commonality that allows Reggie to see into Cohle's future. It also carries a more far-reaching implication – that there is an unseen script, a supernatural narrative that only members of the Yellow King cult can access.

At first Cohle is unimpressed by Reggie's rambling. "What is that?" He asks, barely paying attention. "Nietzsche? Shut the fuck up."[19] But the prophecy weighs on Cohle, growing more significant and troublesome as the years wear on. Rather than ignore Reggie's strange ideas, he internalizes them. In 2012, Cohle mentions Reggie's ideas as fact - not prophecy - during his interview with Detectives Gilbough and Papina saying, "everything we've done or will do we're going to do over and over again."[20] Though there is no connection between Cohle and the cult of the Yellow King cult at the outset of the narrative, Reggie's Carcosa prophecy manipulates Cohle into *building* a connection. Cohle gives the prophecy significance and adopts it as part of his own world view. As the investigation continues, Cohle is faced with an unsettling notion. If Childress is acting as the author of this murder play, then Cohle may not be investigating Dora Lange's murder of his own free will; perhaps he is being manipulated into playing out a role scripted for him by a malevolent author.

> The face you wear is not your own. The shape of our true face is not yet known to us.
> — Joel Theriot

The motif of masks and unmasking is pervasive in *True Detective*. The most obvious examples are literal masks, like the animal masks and hoods worn by the Tuttle family as they celebrate their "very rural sense of Mardi Gras,"[21] and the Chtulu-esque gas mask worn by Reggie Ledoux as he stalks around his property with a machete. Initially, these literal masks seem to serve the traditional purpose in the narrative: hiding an individual's face and obscuring

---

[18] *True Detective*. "The Secret Fate of All Life." Episode 5. Directed by Cary Joji Fukunaga. Written by Nic Pizzolatto. HBO. February 16, 2014.
[19] Ibid.
[20] Ibid.
[21] *True Detective*. "After You've Gone." Episode 7. Directed by Cary Joji Fukunaga. Written by Nic Pizzolatto. HBO. March 2, 2014.

his identity from other characters and the audience. However, by the time Marty Hart and Rust Cohle see these masked villains, the detectives already have a good idea of who is behind the masks. Hart and Cohle can deduce that Reggie Ledoux is behind the gas mask because they followed his brother Dewall Ledoux to the compound where they see the masked man. Similarly, the detectives are confident that the masked men who abuse and murder Marie Fontenot are members of the Tuttle family, because Cohle went to great lengths to steal video evidence of the event from Reverend Tuttle's personal safe and they already have statements linking the Tuttle family to ritual murder. Physical masks in *True Detective* prove ineffective at hiding the identity of criminal suspects, instead functioning more as confirmation of what the detectives already suspected. In this way, the traditional purpose of a mask is reversed; it gives identity to characters rather than obscuring it.

Literal masks appear only on Yellow King cult members, but the metaphorical wearing of masks is not limited to a single character or set of characters in *True Detective*. If anything, wearing figurative masks is presented as a quintessentially human activity. Multiple characters mask parts of their personalities in order to play out the roles expected of them by society. Marty and Maggie Hart wear the masks of "family man" and "devoted wife," but in private they remove their public masks and don the masks of people trapped in an unhappy marriage.[22] Cohle hides his existential anxiety and grief over the loss of his daughter by wearing the mask of an erudite and unflinchingly logical detective. He exchanges that mask for another when he infiltrates the Iron Crusaders and wears his old undercover identity, "Crash." The frequency with which characters don and remove their masks highlights the manufactured and transient nature of identity.

Maggie, Marty and Cohle are all aware, to some extent, that they are characters playing out roles required by the society in which they live. Hart is quick to list the different types of detective he has seen on the job in his 2012 interview with Detectives Gilbough and Papina. Maggie rebels against the idea that she is a character, telling her mother "I think you need to stop confusing

---

[22] Like *True Detective*, "The Mask" features a love triangle between friends. In Chamber's story the sculptor Boris and his friend Alec both pursue the affection of Genevieve. She remains close to both men but chooses Boris as her lover. Heartache and calamity ensue.

me with your soap operas."[23] Cohle, however, finds this awareness terrifying and perverse, citing the works of pessimist philosophers who have taken the idea of malleable identity to its logical and disturbing conclusion. Cohle parrots these ideas by stating, "we are things that labor under the illusion of having a self... when in fact everybody's nobody."[24] A mask does not hide a person's true face; it merely hides his emptiness.

The panic that Cohle feels about malleable identities echoes the unease around masks and unmasking in Chambers's work. In "The Mask," another of the stories from *The King in Yellow*, Chambers includes a quote from the forbidden play wherein two women speak with a mysterious stranger:

> **Camilla:** You, sir, should unmask.
> **Stranger:** Indeed?
> **Cassilda:** Indeed, it's time. We all have laid aside disguise but you.
> **Stranger:** I wear no mask.
> **Camilla:** *(terrified, aside to Cassilda)* No mask? No mask![25]

The King in Yellow-inspired mask motif in *True Detective* is most apparent in the character of Errol Childress.[26] The burn scars around Errol's mouth and jaw are pale and waxy, reminiscent of the "pallid mask" associated with a servant of *The King in Yellow* named The Stranger (as referenced in the quote above). Like other characters in *True Detective*, Childress wears a mask to function in society – that of a simple maintenance man[27] – but unlike the other characters in *True Detective*, he actually removes his mask.

---

[23] *True Detective*. "Seeing Things." Episode 2. Directed by Cary Joji Fukunaga. Written by Nic Pizzolatto. HBO. January 19, 2014.

[24] *True Detective*. "The Long Bright Dark." Episode 1. Directed by Cary Joji Fukunaga. Written by Nic Pizzolatto. HBO. January 12, 2014.

[25] Chambers, Robert W. *The King in Yellow*. New York, NY: Fall River Press, 2014.

[26] Some fans have taken Errol's explicit connections with Yellow King cult in *True Detective* to mean that he is, in fact, *the* Yellow King or *the* King in Yellow. As evidence of their theory, these fans cite that the names Cassilda and Camilla appear scrawled on the walls of Childress's "daddy's cabin," (episode 8, "Form and Void") a direct reference to the play version of The King in Yellow. Additionally, they cite Childress's first on-screen appearance in episode 3, "The Locked Room" as a clue to his true identity. If the scene is paused at just the right time, one of the poles from a chain link fence bifurcates the sign out front of the school, changing the message on it from "school closed / until furth r notice / god is working" to "notice / king."

[27] "The Repairer of Reputations" mentions a maintenance worker outside of a church, describing him as riding "...a lawn mower, dragged by a fat white horse."

The horror of an unmasked face is foreshadowed when detective Cohle visits Kelly, the girl who survived horrific abuse at the Ledoux compound. She implicates Errol Childress as one of her abusers by whispering, "the man with the scars was the worst."[28] When pressed for details about the scarred man, Kelly becomes hysterical, screaming, "His face! His face! His face!"[29] Kelly's reaction echoes Camilla's terror at seeing the Stranger's face in The King in Yellow play excerpt. Much like the Stranger, Childress's unmasked face is nothingness, oblivion, a complete lack of identity so unfathomable that the human mind breaks when forced to behold it. That horror, however, is not unique to Childress. It's an emptiness that could be lurking behind the mask of every other character in *True Detective*, but Errol Childress is the only character perverse enough to remove his mask and reveal the howling void inside himself.

The mask motif carries through to the climactic sequence where Childress lures Cohle into the crumbling stone labyrinth he calls Carcosa. Cohle enters Carcosa wearing the mask of a man seeking justice, a man looking to repay a debt, but the Yellow King's realm is not a place for the manufactured masks of human identity. Carcosa is a place to shed the illusion of having a self and accept the horrible truth that "everybody's nobody."[30] A complete nullification of the self is what Errol Childress demands when he bellows, "take off your mask!"[31]

> Him who eats time. Him robes... it's a wind of invisible voices.
> — Miss Delores

The idea of insignificance, of total erasure by an entity so powerful it can't be comprehended, lies at the heart of cosmic horror. In *The King in Yellow* Robert W. Chambers created a figure emblematic of that terror. The King in

---

This detail from Chambers's story is a possible inspiration for Childress's occupation and the memorable scenes of him on a riding mower outside of public buildings.
[28] *True Detective*. "Haunted Houses." Episode 6. Directed by Cary Joji Fukunaga. Written by Nic Pizzolatto. HBO. February 23, 2014.
[29] Ibid.
[30] *True Detective*. "The Long Bright Dark." Episode 1. Directed by Cary Joji Fukunaga. Written by Nic Pizzolatto. HBO. January 12, 2014
[31] *True Detective*. "Form and Void." Episode 8. Directed by Cary Joji Fukunaga. Written by Nic Pizzolatto. HBO. March 9, 2014.

Yellow is the very essence of the uncanny. With only a few key details to define him, The King in Yellow becomes a spirit that can permeate innumerable new stories. The fluidity of the King, his Yellow Sign, and Carcosa become a twisted Rorschach test that allows the audience to become fascinated with terrors of their own creation. Seeking to identify The King in Yellow removes the mystery of the character, turning eerie menace to quotidian crime. Horror thrives in the shadows, not in the flashbulb glare of a mugshot.

Compensating for a Tragic Misstep in Evolution: Zapffe's Strategies for Minimizing Consciousness

During his first of many existential conversations with his partner, Rust Cohle defines himself as "a realist... but in philosophical terms, I'm what's called a pessimist."[1] In addition to making him poor company at parties, Cohle's comment indicates that he has studied philosophy and hints that he may be "drawn to the extreme fringes of philosophical speculation."[2] Pessimist philosophy has some overlap with nihilist and existential schools of philosophy, but it is not as well known. It remains obscure due to its focus on topics most people find disturbing – such as the idea that life is implicitly horrible and

---

[1] *True Detective*. "The Long Bright Dark." Episode 1. Directed by Cary Joji Fukunaga. Written by Nic Pizzolatto. HBO. January 12, 2014.
[2] Patches, Matt. "Ask a Philosopher: What's Up with *True Detective*'s Rust Cohle?" Vulture. February 28, 2014. Accessed September 17, 2018.
http://www.vulture.com/2014/02/philosopher-assesses-true-detective-characters-rust-cohle-marty-hart.html.

humanity should embrace death. When writer Nic Pizzolatto has Cohle mention pessimist philosophy by name in the first episode of the series, he signals to the audience that existential questions will be thematically relevant in *True Detective*.

> So what's the point of getting out of bed in the morning?
> — Marty Hart

Pizzolatto has named several influences for Cohle's philosophical leanings,[3] but Norwegian existentialist Peter Wessel Zapffe's pessimistic views about the nature of human existence and consciousness echo throughout *True Detective*. In his essay, "The Last Messiah," Zapffe defines consciousness as man's ability to know himself as a unique individual coupled with the awareness that like all living beings, he must die. For Zapffe, this self-awareness is a burden rather than a blessing. It is "a biological paradox, an abomination, an absurdity, an exaggeration of disastrous nature."[4] When describing his philosophical views, Cohle clearly shares Zapffe's negative view of self-awareness. "Human consciousness," he informs Hart, "is a tragic misstep in evolution."[5]

Zapffe argues that humanity's overpowered consciousness is a tragedy and that man has become "unfit for life by over-evolving one ability." To illustrate his point, Zapffe makes the analogy that humanity's consciousness is like a heavy rack of antlers on a deer. "In depressive states" he warns, self-awareness

---

[3] In creating the character Rust Cohle, Pizzolatto draws heavily on the work of horror writer Thomas Ligotti, specifically on Ligotti's non-fiction work, *The Conspiracy Against the Human Race: A Contrivance of Horror* (2011, Hippocampus Press). Ligotti's book is a review and analysis of the works of several literary figures and philosophers. Peter Wessel Zapffe's work is foundational to Ligotti's book, but Zapffe's philosophy was written many years before Ligotti's book and not dependent upon Ligotti's analysis. Rather than attempt to examine the influence of Zapffe's ideas through the lens of Ligotti's writing, this essay removes the intermediary and focuses directly on Zapffe's ideas about consciousness as applied to the characters and narrative of *True Detective*. For a detailed look at Ligotti's influence on Pizzolatto and *True Detective*, see Appendix 3 of this volume, "Just the Facts Ma'am."

[4] Zapffe, Peter Wessel. "The Last Messiah." *Philosophy Now*, March/April 2004, 35-39. The first English translation of the classic essay by Peter Wessel Zapffe, originally published in Janus #9, 1933. Translated from the Norwegian by Gisle R. Tangenes.

[5] *True Detective*. "The Long Bright Dark." Episode 1. Directed by Cary Joji Fukunaga. Written by Nic Pizzolatto. HBO. January 12, 2014.

weighs on man just like the over-heavy antlers of the deer, "...all its fantastic splendor pinning its bearer to the ground."[6]

When viewed as a reference to Zapffe's analogy, the crown of horns on Dora Lange's body can be interpreted as a reference to the burden of consciousness. Dora lived a rough life of drug abuse and prostitution, but the existential tragedy is that her self-awareness gave her the ability to see herself as a broken and exploited human being. Ironically, it is Dora's killer who draws attention to her life of suffering and degradation by placing a crown of antlers on her head.

The antlers on Dora Lange's head evoke both Christ's crown of thorns and Zapffe's metaphor for the "burden of consciousness." *True Detective*, season 1, episode 1, "The Long Bright Dark." HBO.

> For a guy who sees no point in existence, you sure fret about it an awful lot... you still sound panicked.
> — Marty Hart

The Dora Lange case and the possible motivations of her killer leave both detectives shaken. Hart goes so far as to describe it as "the most fucked up

---

[6] Zapffe, Peter Wessel. "The Last Messiah." *Philosophy Now*, March/April 2004, 35-39. The first English translation of the classic essay by Peter Wessel Zapffe, originally published in Janus #9, 1933. Translated from the Norwegian by Gisle R. Tangenes.

thing I ever caught."[7] His reaction illustrates another of Zapffe's ideas about consciousness. Namely that it expands man's awareness of suffering and injustice beyond what he personally experiences. Man looks out on the world and sees innocent creatures suffer as they age and sicken in their march toward death. He sees accident, injury, and violence strike down people in the prime of their lives. Zapffe concludes that the ability to comprehend the suffering of all other humans makes its entrance into human consciousness "through the gateway of compassion."[8]

As experienced detectives, Hart and Cohle understand there is no justice to when or where or how a life ends. They see death, abuse, and neglect on a daily basis. Logically their experiences should leave the detectives jaded, but throughout the narrative Hart and Cohle still express compassion for victims and concern for the missing women and children in the bayou. The same self-awareness that enables the detectives to understand themselves as unique human beings and grants them the intellectual ability to solve crimes also condemns them to vicariously experience the suffering of all the victims they are unable to save. Zapffe names this awareness "the brotherhood of suffering" shared "between everything alive."[9]

Paradoxically, it is Hart and Cohle's knowledge of how utterly terrible the world is that compels them to struggle against bleak reality. They attempt to save people from death and suffering because they too feel suffering and fear death. Tragically, the detectives understand that in the long run their efforts are doomed. Every victim they save will still die one day, as will the detectives themselves. There is no heroic act, no bravery, no personal sacrifice that can permanently thwart death. Man's compulsion to act, coupled with the knowledge that all action is futile leads Zapffe to the conclusion that man is "the universe's helpless captive," leaving him in "a state of relentless panic... a feeling of *cosmic panic*."[10]

---

[7] *True Detective*. "The Long Bright Dark." Episode 1. Directed by Cary Joji Fukunaga. Written by Nic Pizzolatto. HBO. January 12, 2014.

[8] Zapffe, Peter Wessel. "The Last Messiah." *Philosophy Now*, March/April 2004, 35-39.

[9] Ibid.

[10] Ibid.

That sounds God fuckin' awful, Rust.

— Marty Hart

If all that is guaranteed in life is suffering and death, it raises an obvious question: why don't more people kill themselves? Surely a swift, painless death would be the preferable alternative to living in a permanent state of cosmic panic. Even if most people are like Cohle and "lack the constitution for suicide,"[11] there is still the question of why people bother trying to accomplish anything. Still, despite the crushing strain of living, humanity survives. How is such a thing possible?

Zapffe's answer to the question is that "most people learn to save themselves by artificially limiting the content of consciousness." He goes on to explain that this repression of unpleasant truths is "virtually constant... and is a requirement of social adaptability and of everything commonly referred to as healthy and normal living."[12] In short, humanity functions by living in a permanent state of denial. According to Zapffe, humanity employs four major types of repression mechanisms to subdue this overabundance of consciousness: isolation, anchoring, distraction, and sublimation.

As Zapffe describes these repressive mechanisms he stresses that they can be both beneficial and detrimental.[13] He returns to the analogy of the deer with

---

[11] *True Detective*. "The Long Bright Dark." Episode 1. Directed by Cary Joji Fukunaga. Written by Nic Pizzolatto. HBO. January 12, 2014.

[12] Zapffe, Peter Wessel. "The Last Messiah." *Philosophy Now*, March/April 2004, 35-39.

[13] The reader should note that most people alive today use Zapffe's repressive mechanisms to minimize existential suffering. It is a mistake to read Zapffe's identification of repressive mechanisms as a moral condemnation of individuals who employ them. Zapffe argues humans are biologically hard-wired to survive and reproduce. Use of repressive mechanisms is critical easing the pain and suffering inherent to existence and a necessary tool for staying alive long enough to reproduce and rear children. Use of repressive mechanisms does not imply that individuals who employ them are weak, stupid, or willfully ignorant. Conversely, the ability to identify repressive mechanisms and consciously eschew them does not make an individual stronger, smarter or in any way better than his peers. In fact, Zapffe makes a point to document his own use of a repressive mechanism while writing his essay. He notes, "The present essay is a typical attempt at sublimation. The author does not suffer, he is filling a page and is going to be published in a journal." (Zapffe, Peter Wessel. "The Last Messiah." *Philosophy Now*, March/April 2004, 35-39.)

its over-heavy rack of antlers to demonstrate how repressive mechanisms can have a positive impact. If the deer, "at suitable intervals, had broken off the outer spears of its antlers," it could avoid being crushed under the weight of its majestic horns. Zapffe posits that the use of repressive mechanisms can trim back some of humanity's excess of consciousness, minimizing the suffering of existence. These gains, however, come at a price. Zapffe argues that by trimming back its consciousness, humanity earns only "... a continuance without hope, a march not *up to* affirmation, but a march across its ever recreated ruins."[14]

In *True Detective*, Cohle gives voice to Zapffe's notion that humanity is doomed to a life defined by a repetition of the same patterns. "Everything we've ever done or will do," he warns, "we're going to do over and over again."[15] In addition to introducing pessimistic ideas about the nature of existence, Cohle serves as a foil for Marty's decidedly un-pessimistic world view. Cohle's comments highlight the Zapffian repressive mechanisms his partner uses to cope with cosmic panic and the way polite society in Vermilion Parish is structured to instill, support, and enforce those same repressive structures.

> I got an idea. Let's make the car a place of silent reflection from now on.
> — Marty Hart

The first repressive mechanism identified by Zapffe is *isolation*. He defines it as "a fully arbitrary dismissal from consciousness of all disturbing and destructive thought and feeling."[16] Isolating and dismissing unpleasant thoughts from one's consciousness is a straightforward way to avoid the mental anguish caused by those thoughts. Hart provides a textbook example of isolation when he chooses not to think about the aging process and his own mortality. He tearfully explains to his wife, "I get the feeling like, I can see forty and it's like I'm the coyote in the cartoons, like I'm running off a cliff, and if I don't look

---

[14] Zapffe, Peter Wessel. "The Last Messiah." *Philosophy Now*, March/April 2004, 35-39.

[15] *True Detective*. "The Secret Fate of All Life." Episode 5. Directed by Cary Joji Fukunaga. Written by Nic Pizzolatto. HBO. February 16, 2014.

[16] Zapffe, Peter Wessel. "The Last Messiah." *Philosophy Now*, March/April 2004, 35-39.

down and keep running, I might be fine."[17]

Isolation, however, is only a temporary solution. Unpleasant truths do not go away simply because people stop thinking about them, nor does the anxiety caused by those truths dissipate due to being ignored. Human consciousness is too strong, too evolved to allow man to ignore the basic fact of his mortality. Hart may be able to act with a younger man's swagger and bravado in public, but in private he admits to his wife, "I think I'm all fucked up."[18]

Zapffe notes that isolation manifests at the societal level as "a general code of mutual silence," or what might be called 'tact,' an unspoken understanding of what is and is not appropriate to discuss openly. Zapffe highlights that this code of silence is particularly focused around protecting children, giving them time to become accustomed to the world, to gain some experience and context before having their illusions of safety and order shattered. This protection, Zapffe argues, comes at a price. "In return, children are not to bother adults with untimely reminders of sex, toilet, or death."[19] This bargain of safety in exchange for silence is a child's first experience with the mechanism of isolation.

Hart's isolation mechanism is put under pressure when he and Cohle discover an underaged prostitute at the "hillbilly bunny ranch." Though he is a womanizer and an adulterer, Hart still wants to believe that girls are chaste until fully mature. According to Hart, a teenaged girl shouldn't know about sex at all, much less sell sex for money. "At that age," he scolds the madam, "she isn't equipped to make those kind of choices."[20] Hart's argument is made on the assumption that the girl came from a safe and loving home. However, the madam reveals that the girl was raised in a place where adults did not isolate children from sex – a reality that Hart does not want to consider.

Perhaps driven by a panic over the inevitable loss of sexual innocence that lies in store for his own daughters, Hart slips some money into the hand of the

---

[17] *True Detective*. "The Locked Room." Episode 3. Directed by Cary Joji Fukunaga. Written by Nic Pizzolatto. HBO. January 26, 2014.
[18] Ibid.
[19] Zapffe, Peter Wessel. "The Last Messiah." *Philosophy Now*, March/April 2004, 35-39.
[20] *True Detective*. "Seeing Things." Episode 2. Directed by Cary Joji Fukunaga. Written by Nic Pizzolatto. HBO. January 19, 2014

teen prostitute and advises her to "do something else."[21] Hart's action may be futile (is a handful of cash really enough to fix everything wrong in the girl's life?), but it allows him to feel good about himself, to safely isolate his worries about the sexual safety of children from the reality of underage prostitution. Cohle, however, sees through Hart's repressive mechanism and calls out the underlying hypocrisy. "Is that a down payment?"[22] he asks, insinuating that Hart will one day have sex with the girl.[23] Cohle's question forces Hart to see beyond the arbitrary wall he has built separating chaste little girls from sexually mature women. In that moment, Hart's isolation fails and he must logically acknowledge that all his sexual conquests were once innocent children like his own daughters.

> Not everybody wants to sit alone in an empty room beating off to murder manuals. Some folks enjoy community... a common good.
> — Marty Hart

Another repressive mechanism Zapffe identified is *anchoring*. He defines it as an attempt to find fixed points within "the liquid fray of consciousness,"[24] an attempt by man to alleviate the anxiety of a chaotic world by mooring himself to unchanging, infallible truths or institutions. The mechanism is in play from earliest childhood when parents, home, and school serve as the monolithic truths in life. A child grounds himself on the notion that his parents will always be there for him, that his home is a place of refuge, and that school will structure the majority of his time. As a child grows he realizes that family, home, and school are, in many ways, as unreliable as anything else in the world. He outgrows these anchoring points and must take up new ones, lest he be lost in a sea of anxiety during the inevitable difficulties and suffering of life.

Zapffe argues that adults find their greatest relief in shared anchoring points. "Any culture is a great, rounded system of anchorings, built on foundational firmaments."[25] Each culture has a set of basic shared values, but there are a few which transcend across cultures. Of these, Zapffe lists God, the

---

[21] Ibid.

[22] Ibid.

[23] Or, as it turns out, making an accurate prediction.

[24] Zapffe, Peter Wessel. "The Last Messiah." *Philosophy Now*, March/April 2004, 35-39.

[25] Ibid.

Church, and morality as the primary values. Religion, government, and moral codes are largely inherited and have been built up over centuries. Any logical flaws in these traditional systems are not subject to critical thinking. If they are noticed at all, they are usually accepted as a small hiccup in a system which generally promotes the common good.

Marty Hart's attitude toward religion provides an excellent example of the power of anchoring. Hart identifies as a Christian, but he regularly commits adultery and blasphemy. The only time he is depicted attending a religious ceremony is when he and Cohle attend The Friends of Christ tent revival as part of their investigation. Though he does not live by the teachings of Christianity and shows no sign of believing in its core tenants, Hart still believes in its value as a firmament for society. "Can you imagine, if people didn't believe, what things they'd get up to?" For Hart, the shared moral anchor of Christianity[26] is all that keeps the good people of Vermilion Parish from devolving into a "freak show of murder and debauchery."[27] Without it, people would have no hope of anything better than suffering and death, and no motivation to adhere to any of the moral codes that help society function.

On first viewing, it is easy to dismiss Hart as a hypocrite, but a closer examination of Hart's interviews with Gilbough and Papina hint at a more complicated relationship between Hart's values and his actions. When speaking with the younger detectives, Hart describes all of Zapffe's repressive mechanisms, not by name but in the form of advice to the younger men.[28] Hart may come across as a good old boy clinging to old fashioned ideals, but he has an instinctual understanding of the utility of traditions. Hart's focus on the value of traditions as codified repressive mechanisms demonstrates one of

---

[26] Note that *any* religion could provide an anchoring point, even worshiping the Yellow King. There is no need for the religion to contain a positive moral code, only that the moral code be shared by a group of people and passed down over generations. Errol Childress goes about his "important work" of sacrificing women and children to the Yellow King hoping that he may escape his life and ascend to the "infernal plane." The worship of the Yellow King also provides Childress with a way to connect with and share in the traditions of the larger Tuttle family. In this sense, worshiping the Yellow King is an anchoring mechanism for Errol Childress just as much as Christianity is an anchoring point for Marty Hart.

[27] *True Detective*. "The Locked Room." Episode 3. Directed by Cary Joji Fukunaga. Written by Nic Pizzolatto. HBO. January 26, 2014.

[28] Note that most of the pull quotes in this chapter are from Marty Hart's dialogue.

Zapffe's most important points, namely that people are often fully aware of the repressive mechanisms they employ to limit consciousness. Hart is a Christian not because of his faith in Christ, but because he understands it provides a moral anchor for himself and his community. When viewed through this lens, Hart is not a self-satisfied hypocrite. He is a man trying every method he knows to repress his consciousness and still failing. He is in the grip of Zapffe's *cosmic panic*.

> Past a certain age, a man without a family can be a bad thing.
> — Marty Hart

Family is another crucial anchoring point, as a child's first understanding of himself as part of a larger society is when he learns he is part of a family unit. His role within the family is one of the most basic pieces of his identity. When the child becomes a man, he is doubly anchored: once to his birth family and again to the new family he creates through marriage and fatherhood. The biological timetable of reproduction, rearing children, and providing food and shelter takes up much of a man's mental and physical energy. He has limited capacity to ponder the implications of human self-awareness and suffering, as well as limited capacity to explore facets of himself that conflict with his familial obligations. Without a family to anchor him in the world, a man can drift into isolation and despair.

At the outset of the narrative, Cohle has already lost his familial anchor twice over. He is estranged from his father and does not even know if his mother is alive. More importantly, Cohle has also lost the family that he built. The tragic death of his daughter and dissolution of his marriage left him completely unmoored. Without familial obligations to anchor him, Cohle spent four harrowing years deep undercover as a "wild man junkie"[29] before suffering a breakdown and resurfacing in Vermilion Parish. The time Cohle spent adrift in a sea of nihilistic violence and drug abuse did nothing to alter his belief in the value of family as an anchoring mechanism. If anything, it gave him a better understanding of what darkness lies ahead when an anchoring mechanism breaks.

---

[29] *True Detective.* "Seeing Things." Episode 2. Directed by Cary Joji Fukunaga. Written by Nic Pizzolatto. HBO. January 19, 2014.

Cohle demonstrates how much he values family when he urges Maggie not to divorce Hart. "Men, women... it's not supposed to work, except to make kids." He tells her, "it's not about you." [30] As iconoclastic as Cohle may be, he still believes in family as an indispensable anchor for children, the best possible way to protect them until they are better equipped to cope with cruel realities of life. The value Cohle places on family is so strong that he believes that Hart's children will be better off with a dysfunctional family than they would with no family at all. Cohle's argument is that Maggie and Marty should ignore the reality of their failed relationship and live a lie for the greater good – exactly the kind of "fairy tale" he sneered at when he said, "if the common good's gotta make up fairy tales then it's not good for anybody."[31]

> See, infidelity is one kind of sin, but my true failure was inattention.
> — Marty Hart

Cohle's advice to Maggie demonstrates a flaw in the system of repressive mechanisms. As Zapffe explains, "we love our anchorings for saving us, but we also hate them for limiting our sense of freedom."[32] To enjoy the peace of mind provided by repressive mechanisms, such as isolation or anchoring, a man must be a hypocrite of sorts. He must ignore any truth which threatens his repressive mechanisms, as it could tear a hole in the firmament and leave him vulnerable to unmitigated suffering. In order to live with the incongruities between his sheltering values and the reality of his life, man turns to *distraction*. Zapffe defines this popular repressive mechanism as limiting consciousness "by constantly enthralling it with impressions."[33]

Life offers an unending variety of distractions to occupy the body and the mind. Hart drinks to distract himself from the horrors of his job while Cohle relies on illegally acquired barbiturates to sleep at night. Setting aside questions of physical addiction, both men are so psychologically dependent on mind-numbing substances that they cannot cope with life's difficulties while sober.

---

[30] *True Detective*. "Who Goes There." Episode 4. Directed by Cary Joji Fukunaga. Written by Nic Pizzolatto. HBO. February 9, 2014.

[31] *True Detective*. "The Locked Room." Episode 3. Directed by Cary Joji Fukunaga. Written by Nic Pizzolatto. HBO. January 26, 2014.

[32] Zapffe, Peter Wessel. "The Last Messiah." *Philosophy Now*, March/April 2004, 35-39.

[33] Ibid.

Cohle admits this to Gilbough and Papina, saying, "there's nothing I can do about it, maybe not today, maybe not tomorrow, but... I'm gonna have a drink."[34]

Hart uses sex to distract himself from his fears about growing older, and seems incapable of ending his adultery, even when his marriage is at stake. He rationalizes his behavior as necessary saying, "you gotta decompress before you can go bein' a family man. What you get into... workin'... you can't have the kids around that."[35] Hart's affairs provide him a sort of mental distraction as well as physical stimulation. The lies and half-truths required to juggle his job, his family, and mistress require a significant amount of his mental energy. The problem with distraction is that it requires continuous effort, but yields no lasting effects. The moment a stimulating activity ends, the despair it repressed comes floating to the surface just as strong as before. As a man ages, his stamina for distracting activity wanes, leaving him closer to death and with fewer tricks to repress his panicked consciousness.

Hart pinpoints the dangers of growing old without proper anchoring or distracting mechanisms in place, warning Gilbough and Papina: "Lotta guys leave the job, cemetery within ten. No family, idle hands. Some advice? You make it out, you stay busy."[36] Though his advice is sound, Hart fails to act on it. His post-retirement life is a lonely commute from his half-empty private investigation firm in the day to frozen dinners and old cowboy movies at night. Cohle's retirement is similarly bleak. Years of drinking and drug abuse have damaged his mind, making it difficult for him to focus on the investigative work he once found so stimulating.

Left to face their own mortality with failed anchoring and distraction mechanisms, Hart and Cohle are in the grips of what Zapffe calls a "life-panic." This is a state where a man has reached the point where suffering and despair are constant and life is sustainable only by great effort. Zapffe notes that in this

---

[34] *True Detective*. "The Long Bright Dark." Episode 1. Directed by Cary Joji Fukunaga. Written by Nic Pizzolatto. HBO. January 12, 2014.
[35] *True Detective*. "Seeing Things." Episode 2. Directed by Cary Joji Fukunaga. Written by Nic Pizzolatto. HBO. January 19, 2014.
[36] *True Detective*. "The Long Bright Dark." Episode 1. Directed by Cary Joji Fukunaga. Written by Nic Pizzolatto. HBO. January 12, 2014.

condition, "death always appears as an escape."[37] The act of suicide is taboo, one of the many subjects repressively isolated from polite conversation, yet it is a logical option for the man who finds the strain of living too great a burden. Zapffe argues that suicide can serve as a final distraction if the man seeks to imbue his death with a greater meaning. If a man could manage a final gesture, or accomplishment, to "die standing up,"[38] then suicide is no longer an act of cowardice or defeat; it is an admirable act of self-sacrifice.

Cohle expresses the Zapffian desire to escape from the suffering of existence when he informs Hart, "My life has been a circle of violence and degradation for as long as I can remember. I'm looking to tie it off."[39] As Hart delves deeper into the evidence Cohle has collected, he too is taken by the idea of paying off the debt he owes, catching the real monster behind the Yellow King killings, and ending his life as a hero rather than as a broken old man. Maggie, who can still read her ex-husband like a book, is suspicious when Hart visits her, asking, "Are you saying goodbye Marty?"[40] Hart responds with a quiet "thank you," that sounds almost like a suicide note.

> It's just one story... the oldest.
> — Rust Cohle

Zapffe's fourth and final remedy against panic is *sublimation*, which differs from the other methods in that it is "a matter of transformation rather than repression."[41] Sublimation is the act of using artistic or intellectual gifts to transform the pain of living into valuable experiences. It is the positive impulse to engage with the more abstract elements of suffering, "fastening on to its pictorial, dramatic, heroic or even comic aspects"[42] and converting them into a deeper understanding or novel representation of the human experience. Zapffe calls out sublimation as the rarest protective mechanism, noting that to focus

---

[37] Zapffe, Peter Wessel. "The Last Messiah." *Philosophy Now*, March/April 2004, 35-39.

[38] Ibid.

[39] *True Detective*. "After You've Gone." Episode 7. Directed by Cary Joji Fukunaga. Written by Nic Pizzolatto. HBO. March 2, 2014.

[40] Ibid.

[41] Zapffe, Peter Wessel. "The Last Messiah." *Philosophy Now*, March/April 2004, 35-39.

[42] Ibid.

on the aesthetic elements of suffering, the worst of a man's panic must be tamed through other mechanisms. In this way, sublimation is a topmost layer of the panic reducing mechanisms, existing only possible when isolation, anchoring, or distraction have been successfully employed.[43]

After their successful and surprisingly non-lethal run through Carcosa, Hart and Cohle are no longer in a state of "life-panic," as they have recovered some of their valuable coping mechanisms. The planning for, execution of, and fallout from their Carcosa run provided them with a stimulating distraction. Their heroic act helped positively anchor Hart and Cohle to their community, and gave Maggie and her daughters the opportunity to reconcile with Hart. Though he cannot have the same anchoring relationship with them as he did before, Hart's tears of gratitude demonstrate how desperately he needed some kind of connection with his family. Hart, in turn offers himself as an anchor for Cohle with the gift of a pack of cigarettes and a joke about getting engaged.

Rust Cohle gains some comfort from accepting Marty Hart as an anchoring point in his life, but by Zapffe's logic both men will remain forever burdened by consciousness. *True Detective*, season 1, episode 8, "Form and Void." HBO.

---

[43] The present essay is an attempt at sublimation. The author does not suffer, for she is filling pages and is going to be published in a book.

After his brush with death Cohle, the unmoored and uncompromising pessimist, finally accepts a relationship with Hart as an anchoring point in his life. This connection provides him with relief and allows him to use sublimation to transform the anxiety and suffering that have burdened him for so long. Cohle shares his suffering – the visceral memory of the love he lost, the security and warmth associated with his daughter and his father. Upon hearing these raw impressions, Hart urges Cohle to use his abundance of consciousness to frame the experience in a new way. Cohle sublimates his pain, turning it into a grand narrative played out by the stars in the night sky. This sublimation of his personal loss grants Cohle a fresh perspective on the struggle of life. His loss becomes more than just pain. It is the opportunity to create a story about the battle between light and dark, thus offering him a brief reprieve from the suffering of existence.

True Detective's upbeat ending has been read as incongruous with the pessimist philosophy which suffuses the rest of the narrative, but when viewed in light of Zapffe's repressive mechanisms, the ending is not so happy. Hart and Cohle find relief from the pain of existence, but any mechanism, even one as complex as sublimation, can only offer temporary results. If Hart and Cohle are alive, they are forever burdened by consciousness, just as the stag is burdened by his overgrowth of antlers. According to Zapffe, death is the sole escape from this tragic misstep in evolution, the "one conquest and one crown, one redemption and one solution."[44] An ending in which Hart and Cohle survive cannot, by Zapffe's logic, be a happy one, for as long as the men live, they must suffer.

---

[44] Zapffe, Peter Wessel. "The Last Messiah." *Philosophy Now*, March/April 2004, 35-39. The first English translation of the classic essay by Peter Wessel Zapffe, originally published in Janus #9, 1933. Translated from the Norwegian by Gisle R. Tangenes.

APPENDICES:

Fulfillment and Closure, Empty Jars to Store This Abstract Shitstorm

The Guide to *True Detective* and Weird Comic Book Fiction

by Adam Stewart and Mark Stewart

In a moment of exquisite bromance, the final scene of HBO's *True Detective* sees Rust Cohle's black shell finally crack. Wounded, his arm round his friend Marty Hart's shoulder for support, Cohle looks up at the stars and expresses a hopeful attitude for the first time in the series, "once there was only dark, if you ask me the light's winning."[1]

That is, until comics scholar and Alan Moore biographer Lance Parkin spotted similarities between the final scenes of *True Detective* and a panel from the closing pages of Moore and Gene Ha's *Top Ten*, strongly suggesting the comic as the inspiration behind Marty and Rust's optimistic send off. The connection is especially clear when you take into account show creator Nic Pizzolatto's claim that Moore and Grant Morrison (perhaps Britain's second most influential comic book scribe after Moore) were the first writers to excite him about the possibilities of storytelling.

Pizzolatto's Moore crib aside, there are a great many comic book tributaries that feed into *True Detective*. While the list presented here is by no means

---

[1] *True Detective*. "Form and Void." Episode 8. Directed by Cary Joji Fukunaga. Written by Nic Pizzolatto. HBO. March 9, 2014.

exhaustive, it is intended to illuminate the thematic and dramatic intent of the show, as well as provide an overview of those works with which *True Detective* most strongly resonates.

A juxtaposition between *True Detective* and a panel from *Top Ten* #8 (June 2000), in which, while Kapela and the commuter face death, they look up at a starry sky. Written by Alan Moore, with art by Gene Ha. © DC Comics.

The Nightmare Factory
Various writers, various artists

To trace the genealogy of *True Detective*'s psychosphere[2] of "aluminum and ash,"[3] you could start with William Faulkner's forays into the dark heart of his home state of Mississippi, *The Sound and the Fury*, and *Absolom! Absolom!,* or you could look to the comic book adaptation of the works of Thomas Ligotti.

---

[2] The concept of the "psychosphere" originates in weird fiction, appearing in the works of authors from H.P. Lovecraft to Bryan Lumley. It is similar to the idea of a collective consciousness, but with more of an occult flavor. It is a space where human thoughts and experiences can be projected and shared with others. Anyone inhabiting this theoretical space is open to influence – and contagion – by projected symbols, myths, and concepts originating from the shared psyche of the group.
[3] *True Detective.* "The Long Bright Dark." Episode 1. Directed by Cary Joji Fukunaga. Written by Nic Pizzolatto. HBO. January 12, 2014.

An adaptation of the short story anthology of the same name, *The Nightmare Factory* features a commentary by Thomas Ligotti and is one of the few attempts to render Ligotti's stories visually. Ligotti's work is peculiarly suited to comic book translation in that his take on horror is strongly conceptual and doesn't rely on visceral scares better suited to other formats. His emphasis on atmosphere over plot is another plus in this regard. Veteran horror-comic artists Ben Templesmith and Ted McKeever's twisted lines and rotten palettes capture the sickness and foreboding that lurks beneath Ligotti's prose. The scripts by Joe Harris and Stuart Moore sensibly steal liberally from the original texts, ensuring that Ligotti's doom-filled voice underpins the book.

The ties between *True Detective* and Ligotti have been discussed at length elsewhere.[4] Ligotti is both a writer of horror fiction and a philosophical pessimist. *True Detective* borrows heavily from Ligotti's writing, in some instances lifting directly from Ligotti's text to inform Rust Cohle's voice. This allows Rust to articulate a frightening worldview that is distinctly Ligotti-esque. Where *The Nightmare Factory* adaptation stands out is in its aforementioned ability to bring a visual dimension to Ligotti's work, a dimension which is echoed in some of the principal stylistic choices made by the show's director, Cary Joji Fukunaga. The show's septic yellow palette for instance, finds a direct correlate in Templesmith and McKeever's color choices, and Rust's blurry hallucinations mesh closely with Templesmith's dreamy brushstrokes.

While it's true to say that those interested in Rust Cohle's philosophy would be better off reading Ligotti's non-fiction writing on philosophy, *The Nightmare Factory*'s comic book incarnation is arguably the *True Detective*'s closest analogue within the comic book medium. It shares its philosophical underpinnings, it builds a similar world, albeit one that's explicitly supernatural, and it feels like a close cousin in terms of aesthetics and atmospherics. *The Nightmare Factory* isn't *True Detective*, but it many ways it might be the next best thing.

From Hell
Alan Moore, Eddie Campbell

Considered by many to be Moore and Campbell's finest work, *From Hell* is less a tale about Jack the Ripper than an effort to unpick the weave of myth and

---

[4] See Appendix 3, "Just the Facts Ma'am."

history. Equal parts unflinching commentary on the evils of Victorian England, police procedural, and metaphysical treatise, it's a heady book, giddying in its scope and seamless in its execution. There are many formal ties between *True Detective* and *From Hell*. Both are concerned with the nature of stories and storytelling, both use fractured time as a narrative device, both are centered on powerful conspiracies, and the hunts for the killers who lurk at their hearts. Perhaps the strongest point of convergence is to be found in Moore and Pizzolatto's villains and their crimes.

Like *True Detective*'s Errol Childress, Dr. William Gull explores the boundaries of space-time through human sacrifice. *From Hell*, chapter 2 (1999). Written by Alan Moore, with art by Eddie Campbell.

> It's like in this universe, we process time linearly forward but outside of our space-time, from what would be a fourth-dimensional perspective, time wouldn't exist, and from that vantage, could we attain it we'd see our space-time would look flattened, like a single sculpture with matter in a superposition of every place it ever occupied.[5]
> — Rust Cohle

Like *True Detective*, *From Hell* forwards the pop-physics notion that time and space can be conceived of as an object, observable in its entirety from a higher dimensional perspective. Rust calls this hyper-structure a *"flat disc,"* while *From Hell* circles around the concept of the *"fourth dimension."* This conception of reality is reflected in the form and content of many of Moore's

---

[5] *True Detective*. "The Secret Fate of All Life." Episode 5. Directed by Cary Joji Fukunaga. Written by Nic Pizzolatto. HBO. February 16, 2014.

works, most conspicuously in his seminal graphic novel *Watchmen*, which incorporates a great deal of visual, thematic and narrative symmetry, resonance and repetition in an effort to foreground the work's unity. A unity which is made explicit within the story by Dr. Manhattan, a super powered being who can see the entire structure of space-time and anything that happens from his particular perspective within it. In other words, he is in direct communion with his own comic book story, his very own two-dimensional hyper-structure. Like us, Dr. Manhattan is capable of reading his tale from beginning to end or, indeed, from end to beginning. Any point within the structure is open to him, just as we can open the comic on any page.

This view of fiction as a two-dimensional story-universe navigable by three dimensional (human) beings can be applied to TV shows just as much as it can be applied to comic books. Rust's description of his universe as "flat" has a philosophically pessimistic edge, but it's also literally true. From our perspective, it is flat, a two-dimensional image on a flat screen. Like Rust, we stand at a distance and judge his world and its inhabitants. Unlike Rust, our perspective is higher, more complete. We can fast forward, rewind, pause, see how everything fits together in a way that Rust never could. Most importantly, from the point of view of *True Detective*'s antagonist, who professes a desire to transcend "the disc in the loop,"[6] and in some sense Rust, who desperately wants to escape the prison that is his life, we can stand outside it, unmoved by its pains and sorrows.

From Hell's villain is Jack the Ripper, a one Dr. William Gull. Like Errol Childress, *True Detective*'s villain, Gull makes grisly efforts to straddle his world through blood sacrifice. In his case, Victorian London's many dispossessed women are his victims. In many ways this is a stock genre trope, the serial killer hoping to be transformed by the act of murder. See everything Thomas Harris has ever written - from the Tooth Fairy's desire to metamorphose into William Blake's Red Dragon to Buffalo Bill's misguided approach to gender reassignment in *The Silence of the Lambs*. The key difference between Harris's repetition of the trope and Moore's use of it is that Dr. Gull succeeds in his quest for transformation. Throughout the book, and culminating in the final chapter, he

---

[6] *True Detective*. "Form and Void." Episode 8. Directed by Cary Joji Fukunaga. Written by Nic Pizzolatto. HBO. March 9, 2014.

literally ascends to a strange vantage point from which he can see across time and space.

As Pizzolatto notes in a post-mortem interview, Errol is trying to achieve something very similar.

> When he [Errol] says, "My ascension removes me from the disc in the loop," he's describing the cosmology of eternal recurrence of various characters, including Cohle and Reggie Ledoux hit upon, and he's hitting upon his personal mythology... He believes the murders ritually enacted over a period of time, upon his death, permit him an ascension that removes him from the Karmic wheel of rebirth.[7]

Here we must stop and consider exactly what Moore thinks he's doing, and whether it has any bearing on Pizzolatto's aims. Very simply, and without wishing to paint the writer as overly eccentric, Moore believes that mythic structures stand outside space and time, and that our world is at some fundamental level composed of these stories. As Moore makes plain in *From Hell*'s must-read appendices, he considers Jack the Ripper to be a modern-day myth, hence Jack/Gull's ultimate ascendance into the ether, where he lives on as the quintessential serial killer narrative of our age. Gull can move through space-time because as a myth he isn't tied to any particular time and place, but rather to the ideas that underpin our world.

Given Pizzolatto's familiarity with Moore, it's reasonable to assume that he knows something about Moore's personal philosophy. After all, Moore isn't shy about coming forward with his views, or indeed setting them out at great length in his fiction. Most notably in *Promethea*, his enormous and popular treatise on the practice of magick cum Wonder Woman riff, and within the pages of *From Hell* itself, with William Gull as the conduit. All of which explains why most of the writer's fans, and many of his detractors, are intimately familiar with Moore's unconventional take on metaphysics and how it ties into fiction via storytelling.

On a literary level, Gull's transcendence illustrates the pervasive power of the myth of Jack the Ripper, but, in light of what we know about Moore, it's quite possible that it is also meant to illustrate a means by which a literal

---

[7] Jensen, Jeff. "*True Detective* Post-mortem: Creator Nic Pizzolatto on Happy Endings, Season 2, and the Future of Cohle and Hart." EW.com. March 10, 2014. Accessed October 12, 2018. https://ew.com/article/2014/03/10/true-detective-post-mortem-creator-nic-pizzoletto-on-happy-endings-season-2-and-the-future-of-cohle-and-hart/.

transcendence is attainable. Which takes us back to Pizzolatto's understanding of his killer, Errol Childress, and the question of whether or not there is any similarity between Gull's transcendence and Childress's methods. Like Gull, Childress surrounds himself with the language of myth. He adopts the voices of golden age movie stars and nurtures a rich seam of iconography through the practice of ritual murder. Moreover, by invoking Robert Chambers's *The King in Yellow* - a story about a mysterious character synonymous with death and destruction, not unlike Jack the Ripper - Pizzolatto brings to bear the idea that some stories have a life of their own and are powerful enough to change the world. It's a point reinforced throughout the narrative by Rust's constant criticism of the stories other characters tell themselves in order to make their lives bearable.

Putting aside Childress's stated goal of transforming himself into a higher-dimensional being, it could be argued that he attains the kind of mythological transcendence described by Moore. Take the image of the flare rising above Carcosa, which comes after the final confrontation between Rust and Childress. It's a beautiful shot, but while some have interpreted this as a moment of hope, it seems unlikely that it was intended that way. Rust is to all intents and purposes, dead and the cavalry has arrived too late, and that's before we consider Childress's belief that he will rise above the disc to the infernal plane as he dies - an event which this imagery directly evokes. The fact that this reading is so apparent isn't simply a product of the heroes' dire circumstances in that instant; it's because the show has established an internal mythological language by which to understand it. Furthermore, it has established that the Childress murders are something of a *cause celebre* in his fictional world. Now that Childress's name can be attached to them, it's reasonable to assume that he'll ascend into the pantheon of serial killers. But there's more, perhaps in revealing his identity to us, the audience, the character also transcends the bounds of his flat television universe, to live on in our minds. Fanciful? Yes, but plausibly something that Pizzolatto was playing with.

Neonomicon
Alan Moore, Jacen Burrows

Some in *True Detective*'s audience were disappointed that the show never leaned into the supernatural horror fiction which informed it. *Neonomicon* is the comic for those fans. Technically two miniseries in one volume, the collected edition discussed here brings together a comic book adaptation of

Alan Moore's prose Lovecraftian horror story *The Courtyard* and a follow up title written directly for the medium by Moore himself, *Neonomicon*. To say that both are an uncomfortable read would be an understatement. Written when Moore was in a "bad mood," *Neonomicon* has been criticized for its graphic depictions of sexual violence. Which isn't to say that *The Courtyard* is light reading, what with its pseudo-nazi protagonist and abundant gore, only that it doesn't feature alien entities engaging in rape.

Other than sex crimes by monsters, *True Detective* and *Neonomicon* share a number of trivial similarities. The first part of *Neonomicon*, *The Courtyard*, features Aldo Sax, a socially alienated lead with extraordinary powers of perception. *Neonomicon* focuses on two murder investigations, each with links to a cult that worships Lovecraftian deities. *Neonomicon* has its own mysterious antagonist, Jonnie Carcosa, with supernatural concerns. *Neonomicon* is a police procedural stocked with odd couple investigating officers. Like *True Detective*, *Neonomicon* blurs genre distinctions by blending detective fiction with a smattering of horror genre tropes, supernatural elements - quasi or otherwise - and questions about the nature of reality. Other examples of this hard to pin down fictional category include *Twin Peaks* and *Blue Velvet*, maybe Grant Morrison's *The Mystery Play*, a restaging of the classic mystery play format for a modern comic book reading audience. Unlike the other works listed here, *True Detective* never commits to any kind of explicitly supernatural presence. Some strangeness bleeds in at the edges, but it's all intimation, all tease. *Neonomicon*, on the other hand, takes many of the horror elements which *True Detective* eschewed and gives them free reign within a framework that shares more than a passing resemblance with HBO's show.

To take one comparison, *True Detective*'s creepy murals don't just depict the mythology of the cult of the Yellow King. They work with Rust's philosophical pessimism and the grim realities of the plot to create a vision of a doomed world. In a sense they allow us to peer into its dark heart, much as Childress no doubt uses them to aid his psychic excursions to the "infernal plane." *Neonomicon* also develops a rich mythology in an effort to create a frightening undertone to everyday reality. Where Pizzolatto roots his conspiracy in history and traditional power structures (politicians, the police, old money), Moore deploys the cultural artifacts and language of another alien group, the young: nightclubs, street fashions, slang, and – yes – strange murals. Contrary to Pizzolatto, Moore intends them to go beyond generating atmosphere or ambiguous gestures towards the supernatural.

Early in *Neonomicon*, Jonnie Carcosa escapes the police by disappearing into a graffiti mural, which is ultimately revealed to be a portal to another dimension. While *True Detective* offers us insight into Childress's psychopathic reality through its attendant mythological trappings, *Neonomicon* literally takes us there. This isn't a superficial comparison when you consider that both are interested in how myths - stories - can change the world, or at least how it's understood. By moving into the painting, Moore is suggesting, via Carcosa, that art, in particular this frightening art, has just as much to say about the bedrock of our existence as the physical. An idea that's unpacked and made explicit in both texts in a variety of ways, most notably through the use of autocritical devices. In *True Detective*, Pizzolatto uses Rust to deconstruct the upbeat stories the other characters tell themselves in an effort to showcase a darker story that lies beneath (one which will ultimately be supplanted by another, more positive story), a space figuratively occupied by the mythological landscape of Childress and his Yellow King. In *Neonomicon*, Moore presents us with a drug made of language - an alien language to be precise - that gives its users access to gruesome truths that are obscured by our human linguistic constructions. Part of the connective tissue here is, of course, insanity and murder, which arises in both the show and the comic as a natural outcome of interfacing with the terrible truths underlying reality.

Another conceptual thread that runs deep in *True Detective* and *Neonomicon* is the thought that time is an illusion and that the world is better understood as a multidimensional structure. In *Neonomicon*, this has consequences for the plot, albeit one of a more explicitly science fictional bent, in that there really are monstrous beings who lurk outside the space-time object where *Neonomicon* is set, the human universe/"Leng." Interestingly, while *True Detective* sees its villain attempt to exit our world by rising above "the disc in the loop,"[8] the monsters of *Neonomicon* are looking to go the other way and descend upon Earth. Both texts reify their fictional worlds, and through this process of presenting them as objects, ascribe attributes to them. In both cases, the predominant attribute, which the show and comic go to great pains to reinforce, is an existential sickness. For Childress and Rust, the disc in the loop is a world of pain and suffering to be escaped or mastered. For

---

[8] *True Detective.* "Form and Void." Episode 8. Directed by Cary Joji Fukunaga. Written by Nic Pizzolatto. HBO. March 9, 2014.

Neonomicon's protagonist, Agent Brears, her "bullshit" world is populated by human "vermin," a point bolstered by the comic's relentlessly grim tone and bloody violence. The forthcoming apocalypse posited as a necessary cleansing rather than an outcome to be feared, although one gets the impression that everyone other than Agent Brears has a lot to worry about, at least in the short term. Lovecraft's gods are not known for their gentleness.

Heading back into Ligotti territory, this sense of there being something intrinsically wrong with human existence is unequivocally philosophically pessimistic, and it's here that *Neonomicon* and *True Detective* find the most common ground. While it's fun to dwell on the interplay between the two texts in terms of horror tropes and literary throughlines, the genuinely horrific worlds in which Rust and Brears find themselves are, at root, what these stories are about. With that in mind, *True Detective* and *Neonomicon* can feel as if they are entirely dedicated to worldbuilding until their final moments. Evil is piled on top of evil until critical mass is reached and both stories offer up alternative sites of meaning in the form of wider fictional realities. Realities, whose introduction is prefaced by scenes where the protagonists have a visionary experience that underlines the limits of their respective perspectives. Rust sees a vision of his "flat disc," Brears catches a glimpse of Leng. The tacit assertion in each case is that the grim universes that they inhabit are not the totality, that something more is possible. In this view, pessimism is presented as yet another chauvinistic philosophical construct, perhaps applicable to some aspect of existence but not the whole.

On the surface, Moore and Pizzolatto appear to go in very different directions with this idea. In the case of *Neonomicon*, the totality is bigger and better precisely because the human world is an insignificant one, soon to be crushed part of it. In *True Detective*, the wider world is one where goodness is a possibility. Where the texts noticeably intersect is through the idea that these worlds will only become truly accessible to their protagonists after a process of physical and psychological transformation, a process with the traditional hallmarks of an occult initiation into the universe's mysteries, and another subject dear to Moore's heart. Rust experiences this transformation in the form of severe injury and a near-death hallucination involving his father and daughter, Brears experiences something similar through pregnancy and childbirth. Key to both instances is an encounter with that most life-changing feature of human existence - in fiction, at least - parenthood. Admittedly, for Brears her child's birth will amount to the dawn of the apocalypse, but in fairness to Moore's "bad mood," childbirth often involves rebuilding our lives from the ground up. In that light, maybe *Neonomicon* only seems like a horror story - just like *True Detective*.

Mister Miracle
Grant Morrison, Pascal Ferry

On the face of it, Grant Morrison and Pascal Ferry's *Mister Miracle* doesn't have a lot in common with *True Detective*. A high octane, psychedelic super hero adventure that sits within the broader *Seven Soldiers* miniseries, *Mister Miracle* tells the story of Shilo Norman, a super escape artist who battles to free the world from the clutches of a dark god. Dig deeper, however, and things start to get interesting. Like Rust, Shilo is trapped in a "flat disc" reality up until the final minutes of the story, albeit a black hole rather than *"matter in superposition."* Both Rust and Shilo are held prisoner, or at least consider themselves held prisoner, in a *"life trap,"*[9] an endless cycle of meaningless lives. Both are haunted by the loss of a loved one they couldn't save. Rust uses this very term, as does Boss Dark Side, Mister Miracle's diabolic antagonist.

Boss Dark Side and Childress each present us with a vision of a world of pain and suffering that the hero must overcome if they're to move on with their lives. In *Mister Miracle* this conflict is literal. In one memorable scene, Shilo must fend off attacks by demonic cars; in another, he's tortured to death by plastic men with bolt cutters. In true comic book fashion, Boss Dark Side's ultimate weapon, Omega, isn't merely a nasty lens through which to view reality, it's a sentient life-story that seals its prey behind bars of misery and hopelessness. The only way to defeat it is to come to terms with it - an actual conversation - and offer up a better story, one that includes the possibility of forgiveness.

This competing story dynamic cuts to the heart of *True Detective*, as Rust serves an autocritical function. His profoundly reductive point of view shines an unforgiving light on the stories that make up *True Detective*'s world, be they Marty's tales about family and masculinity, Reverend Theriot's brand of religious revivalism, or Rust's very own cathartic narratives, which is what he calls the tools he uses to extract confessions from criminals. The trick the show plays is to fool the viewer into thinking that Rust's take, while horrible, has a

---

[9] *True Detective.* "The Locked Room." Episode 3. Directed by Cary Joji Fukunaga. Written by Nic Pizzolatto. HBO. January 26, 2014.

Mister Miracle stars Shilo Norman, an escape artist who battles to free the world from the clutches of a dark god. *Seven Soldiers: Mister Miracle* #1 (September 2005). Written by Grant Morrison, with art by Pasqual Ferry. © DC Comics.

firmer hold on the show's reality than anyone else's. It does this in a number of ways. McConaughey's considerable charm is a significant start in making Rust a persuasive character. Rust is also presented as a man who has little if anything to gain by being right. Unlike Marty, who actively benefits from his personal fictions in that they mask or legitimize his bad behavior, at least in the short term. More subtly, the show works to reinforce the dominance of Rust's worldview by aligning it with the iconography and philosophy of the villain's, thereby lending it an all pervasive, quasi-supernatural authority.

Of course, the apparent objectivity of Rust's worldview is ultimately undermined and reframed as yet another cathartic narrative. In his case, designed to lessen the pain and guilt he carries in the wake of his daughter's death. In his original recounting, her passing is a blessing, an escape from "the sin of being a father."[10] But ultimately, Rust, like Shilo, finds himself face to face with a competing story he can't overcome. In the darkness - for Rust a coma, for Shilo an encounter with Omega in the heart of the black hole - both characters encounter the love and, implicitly, forgiveness. Consequently, all the talk of life traps, and Omega and flat discs and Carcosa start to look very shaky. Other possibilities present themselves, other stories, like the hope that Rust and Marty can truly be friends, or that Shilo can free himself of the guilt that's dominated his life. Worlds where, to quote Rust, the "light is winning."[11]

Intriguingly, Reverend Theriot's sermon in the *True Detective*'s third episode presents us with an alternative, positive spin on reality, one which echoes the worldview Rust adopts in the closing moments of the show. However, the cut that aired positions Theriot's speech firmly in the background, thereby largely obscuring its content. An alternative edit that foregrounds Theriot's sermon can be found on the HBO's Youtube channel.[12]

---

[10] *True Detective*. "Seeing Things." Episode 2. Directed by Cary Joji Fukunaga. Written by Nic Pizzolatto. HBO. January 19, 2014.

[11] *True Detective*. "Form and Void." Episode 8. Directed by Cary Joji Fukunaga. Written by Nic Pizzolatto. HBO. March 9, 2014.

[12] HBO. "Amen." YouTube. January 24, 2014. Accessed October 13, 2018. https://www.youtube.com/watch?v=5_y5AcBVOx0&feature=youtu.be.

Starting from top left: Jack Frost, Lord Fanny, Boy, King Mob, and Ragged Robin. Cover art for *The Invisibles, Volume Two* #1 (Feb 1997). Art by Brian Bolland. © Vertigo / DC Comics.

The Invisibles

Grant Morrison, various artists

Finally, we arrive at what is in all likelihood the show's biggest conceptual inspiration, Grant Morrison's magnum opus and the benchmark by which his work continues to be judged, *The Invisibles*. For those of you out there who enjoy *True Detective*, but who haven't yet explored this particular metaphysical rabbit hole, it might be time to bite the bullet and give it a try. I warn you though, *The Invisibles* is not for the faint-hearted. The comic's frequently smug tone, its slightly naff fascination with all things Britpop, its disinterest in tying up loose ends, not to mention the fact that one of its characters, a supercool bondage assassin terrorist, is clearly intended as an analogue for the author himself, are enough to scare off many readers midway through the first volume, but persist with it and *The Invisibles* emerges as a "difficult" work of a most rewarding kind.

Roughly speaking, *The Invisibles* tells the story of an occult war raging behind the scenes of The World We Know, with two possibly equally evil secret organizations vying for control of human destiny and the planet. Specifically, the comic focuses on the events of the war's final decade and follows a cell of activists working on behalf of one of the aforementioned creepy conspiracies, the Invisibles, comprising a transvestite shaman, a time displaced witch, a potty-mouthed messiah from Liverpool, a revenge driven ex-cop and Grant Morri-- I mean a super dangerous, kill-crazy bondage assassin. Along the way, it incorporates everything from cutting edge pop-science, to 1970s sci-fi, to Karl Marx, to medieval Sufism, which means it's a very mixed bag indeed. So, if you're tempted to pick it up, get ready for some very abrupt scene shifting and a whole lot of meta-textual references. Having said that, most *True Detective* fans probably don't mind their entertainment flaunting its influences. However, it's not just via their ever-expanding frontiers that these two artworks meet, but also via the subject matters which define their hazy and grasping borders. It's fair to say that *The Invisibles* shares many of *True Detective*'s concerns, themes, symbols, and tropes, but before it hands them off to other authors, it runs with them about as far as it can go.

Psychic detectives investigating occult conspiracies? Look no further than Division X. Black suns? The eclipse door at the end of the comic's third volume. Spaghetti monsters? The Moonchild. Raggedy demons conjured out of old drapes and bone? The Archons. Wicker man-style animal mask wearing, child sacrificing bad guys? Covered. Pagan rituals and time magic? Yes, and yes again. But the connections run deeper than just window dressing.

> Whatever else you may think, you are machines. Biological Robots, operated by electrical firing and chemical spasms.... You in your chaotic state may experience our efforts in value laden terms; feelings of degradation, shame and humiliation are common. Those states are simply

the reaction of a damaged subjective unit during its return to the objective reality of the machine. "Individuality" is the name you give your sickness.[13]

Thus speaks Mr. Quimper, the mind controlling incubus who plagues *The Invisibles* throughout volume two. You could be forgiven for confusing the guy with Rust Cohle. There are two philosophical strands warring within the comic's pages: the expansive and anarchic paradigm of the Invisibles and the mechanistic and socially Darwinian worldview espoused by their opposite, the Outer Church, of whom Quimper is an agent. Tragically, up until *True Detective*'s final curtain, the same could be said of Rust.

Mister Six, member of Division X. *The Invisibles, Volume Three* #11 (Mar 1999). Written by Grant Morrison, with art by Philip Bond. © Vertigo / DC Comics.

Horror and misery are central to *True Detective*'s atmosphere, but *The Invisibles* can be that way too. All you have to do is decide the Outer Church is correct. Seen from the Outer Church's gloomy perspective, the world and all its discontents manifest not dissimilarly from Rust and Ligotti's threshing machine analogy discussed above. It's dressed up in cosmic sci-fi imagery, but what is the terrible future promised by the Outer Church, where 'the beasts inherit the

---

[13] Morrison, Grant and various artists. *The Invisibles Omnibus*. New York, NY: DC Comics, 2012.

Earth' and humanity is herded into 'pens' like cattle in an 'infinite death camp of tomorrow,' other than a metaphor for our simply giving into the animal side of our nature and submitting to extinction?

For *The Invisibles'* most committed enemy, Sir Miles Delacourt, just as with Rust, all of the truths we hold dear are manifestly hollow and empty. Human progress is just an empty lie. As Miles explains to his Invisible opposite seconds before killing him: "Beyond this there are no aeons. There is no evolutionary process. There is only the machine forever and everywhere."[14] Religion, too, is another false panacea. In *True Detective* Rust describes religion as a virus, and while it's not explicitly denigrated in these terms within *The Invisibles*, the accusation is certainly there. The comic often refers to language and ideas in viral and bacterial terms, and was one of the first popular narratives to introduce the meme to the general public. It's easy to infer what the Outer Church's earthly agents, the Myrmidons, would make of the elaborate conceptual palaces erected by the faithful. Sir Miles, though, would understand religion not simply as a virus, but as a highly adaptive super-resistant strain. He goes further and understands all our thoughts that way, right down to the biggest delusions of all: free will and an individual, integral self.

> You're not bad, it's not you. There's a weight and it's got its fish-hooks in your soul.... It's not you. You were dragged to the bottom by that same weight. Listen to me, son: you've got one way out and it's by the grace of God...... You, me, people, we don't choose to feel our feelings. There is grace in this world and there is forgiveness, but you have to ask for it.[15]
> — Rust Cohle

I find Rust's confessionals to be amongst the show's creepier scenes. The way he creates such a high degree of intimacy between himself and the individual he seeks to destroy. It runs deeper than straightforward violence, it's like he wants to touch souls with his victims before pulling away and seeing them consigned to the flames. Except that Rust doesn't believe in souls. For all its religious (read: Southern) trappings, Rust is describing a universe bereft of a director. There is no choice, just the dead weight of history dragging us where it will and the God invoked is an absent one. How can we achieve redemption

---

[14] Ibid.
[15] *True Detective*. "The Locked Room." Episode 3. Directed by Cary Joji Fukunaga. Written by Nic Pizzolatto. HBO. January 26, 2014.

without free will? All that is left for us is to make peace with chaos and our inner robot, to forgive ourselves, a self which is, as Rust explains in the first ten minutes of the very first episode, nothing more than an illusion.

These ideas find an oblique but disturbing correlate in *The Invisibles'* story arc, "American Death Camp," during which Boy, an ex-cop and peculiarly vengeful Invisible, has her personality taken apart by enemy agents adept at psychic warfare. Some readers interpret Morrison's reduction of Boy to a selfless zero as a tacit admission that he didn't know what to do with the team's only black member; and that may be true, but the way he goes about it is horrifyingly effective nevertheless. After being abducted by the enemy cell, Boy's sense of personhood is shattered by the revelation that her current identity is a cover story within a cover story within a cover story, within which her true self has become trapped. The memories of each of these lives are somehow stimulated into re-emerging simultaneously and the ontological shock which ensues softens her up for the final blow. There is a real 'Boy' underneath all these layers and it's anything but human. The comic depicts it as a horrifying bug, its tendrils hooked into Boy's central nervous system.

Rust Cohle uses his crafting skills to explain the shape of the universe and the futility of man's existence. *True Detective*. "The Secret Fate of All Life." Episode 5. Directed by Cary Joji Fukunaga. Written by Nic Pizzolatto. HBO. February 16, 2014.

Boy's sense of personhood is a visceral and near-perfect metaphor for everything Rust describes. What we call consciousness doesn't belong to us. It's something else, from outside, an aggregate of warring memes, nothing more than a monstrous parasite, and our bodies are slaves to its will. This is the philosophical pessimist's take in a nutshell. There is no meaning. There is no creator. There are no souls. All that is left from us is to stagger around blindly in the dark.

I guess you couldn't find a better symbol for the abject awfulness of it all than a wizened alcoholic christening his can of Lone Star "the Universe," before flattening it out and chucking it in the trash. Life's pretty bad when the only things that carry any meaning for you are dead bodies and rubbish beer. That's bottom, surely? Turns out it isn't.

Rust isn't just reducing the universe to poison and garbage, he's also explaining exactly why in his view things are so bad. It's not simply that human beings are damaged subjective units, it's that reality itself is evil. The game was rigged from the start.

> It's a problem of geometry... In our subjective universe we experience three dimensions of space and one of time. However I believe time, like space, has more than one dimension. Think of timespace as a multi-dimensional, self-perfecting system in which everything that has ever, or will ever, occur, occurs simultaneously. I believe timespace is a kind of object, a geometrical supersolid."[16]
> — Takashi Satoh

In both the Invisibles' and Rust's conception, Space-time is an object, which means that every moment, from the universe's alpha to its omega, is happening *right now*. This entails that time, as we perceive it, is an illusion and to someone or something outside of this reality, all of our joys and our sorrows would be arrayed alongside each other like the events in a comic or a beer can flattened out so that its sides and top end are present simultaneously.

What Rust is hung up on is the sorrowful part of the equation. Forget the joys or even the most banal aspects of our lives like doing the shopping, hanging out with our friends or going to the toilet; for Rust, a man who lost his daughter, it's all about the pain. Because Rust can't see past the fact that all our miseries are eternal, he's understandably depressed. Towards the end of *The Invisibles*, Sir Miles is introduced to a maxim which neatly sums up this dreary worldview (one that inverts Hassan Sabbah's and the Invisibles' famous credo):

---

[16] Morrison, Grant and various artists. *The Invisibles Omnibus*. New York, NY: DC Comics, 2012.

"Everything is true, nothing is permitted." In other words, everything that can happen has happened, and there's no changing it. Rust and Miles inhabit a hard deterministic universe, one of pulverizing pointlessness, the sheer weight of which crushes all their hopes and dreams underfoot. It's a universe in which there is no room to act, even to breathe, and sees both of them committing what amounts to slow motion suicide. Miles with his dark gods and black magic, Rust with his drink.

> The body is not one member, but many. Now are they many, but of one body.[17]
> — Rust Cohle

> If our words are circles, theirs are bubbles.[18]
> — Jack Frost

One of the implications of all events existing within the same hyper-moment is that all flesh does too. That all of us are, literally, in some way physically connected to our entire past and future. Not only that, because we all stem from someone else, right back to the first single celled organism which spawned the human race and preceding that the planet, stars and big bang/crunch which birthed and ultimately will end it all, it turns out we're connected to everything else as well. The tree of life isn't metaphor - we're all branching out from the central stem of closely packed matter at the dawn of time. This reality, which on the surface appears so complicated, is in the end just a simple bifurcating program. If we could only see it from the outside, we'd see patterns reproducing themselves with slight variations at different scales across its multidimensional mass, like the twigs or leaves on a tree. Key to understanding Morrison's work, this idea is expressed throughout *The Invisibles*, especially towards the end, where characters who have transcended normal space-time conditions re-emerge as elongated worms with their pasts and futures extending behind and in front of them. A time-lapsed display similar to the visual effects in the video for Amii Stewart's "Knock on Wood." There is a similarity here with *True Detective*'s Lovecraftian 'spaghetti monster', both in

---

[17] *True Detective*. "Seeing Things." Episode 2. Directed by Cary Joji Fukunaga. Written by Nic Pizzolatto. HBO. January 19, 2014.
[18] Morrison, Grant and various artists. *The Invisibles Omnibus*. New York, NY: DC Comics, 2012.

terms of what the name evokes visually, and given that Lovecraft's monstrosities traditionally hail from outside space and time.

> The day-to-day life of the elderly, like that of the magician, is filled with an extraordinarily high level of coincidence.[19]
> — Lady Edith Manning

This concept of an underlying structure to space-time is echoed in the events of *True Detective*. The question is, how literally are we meant to take it? Why does Rust see the birds form the swirling tattoo just prior to discovering the creepy murals in the rundown church? Why does he smell aluminum at both the investigation's beginning and its end? Does the child murderer, Ledoux, who first introduces the idea of flattened-out time circles – or - whatever really know what's going to happen next? After all, a black star does rise - a bullet wound right through his head. If Nic Pizzolatto is familiar with Morrison's work, then it's likely that an *Invisibles* reading of these events is built in and actively encouraged. What would that look like? Well for a start, all this talk of predestination and prognostication wouldn't just be empty words, some of these characters might be able to stand outside of time and witness the recurring patterns. Rust and the murderer's awareness really can track backwards or forwards along the worm.

> You see, man will not be man.... he will be like them.... star-headed.... in the 2012.... the trans continuum... Like the Old Ones! Like *them*![20]
> — Sir Miles Delacourt

> You couldn't look at my face.[21]
> — The Harlequin

> His face, his *faaaaaaaace*![22]
> — Kelly

---

[19] Ibid.

[20] Ibid.

[21] Ibid.

[22] *True Detective*. "Haunted Houses." Episode 6. Directed by Cary Joji Fukunaga. Written by Nic Pizzolatto. HBO. February 23, 2014.

Ragged Robin transcends normal space-time and re-emerges as an elongated worm with her pasts and futures extending behind and in front of her. *The Invisibles, Volume Three* #1 (June 2000). Written by Grant Morrison, with art by Frank Quietly. © Vertigo / DC Comics.

The Yellow King in *The Invisibles* is an amalgamation of two Lovecraftian entities - the King in Yellow[23] and Nyarlathotep. Both characters have at one time or another been rationalized by various contributors to the Cthulhu Mythos, the inspiration for much of the comic's cosmology, as messengers, or avatars, of the fifth dimensional intelligence(s) lurking in wait beyond ordinary, time-bound human perception. They're the inhuman face of this frightening reality. In other words, a bridge between us and it, and Morrison finds clever ways of working this idea into his story.

Much is made, for instance, of the Stranger's famous line from Robert W. Chamber's *The King in Yellow.* In the play a woman asks the Stranger to take off his mask, and he responds "Madam, I wear no mask!"[24] In *The Invisibles*, this same line emerges at a key point in the narrative: the debonair Invisible Mr. Six's defection to the Outer Church. In this scene, after explaining to Six that he can't make the transition without putting aside all his 'cover personalities', the King reiterates the point that his face and his 'mask' are one and the same, only in this instance his words take on a metaphysical dimension. The figure of the King - with his veiled mask, here equated with our own egos, our 'cover personalities' - becomes symbolic of the idea that human consciousness cannot penetrate the beyond - to do so one has to abandon the self entirely. Six's act of betrayal, his union with everything he is not, the Outer Church, affects his own transformation from bounded man to fourth dimensional spaghetti monster. A journey which mirrors Childress's efforts to ascend "the disc in the loop"[25] in the presence of *True Detective*'s King in Yellow, and which resonates with Childress's exhortation to Rust, "take off your mask."[26] Of course Childress's method of transcendence involves darker methods than those laid out in the scene with Mr. Six. An utter betrayal of all things most humans hold dear: murder.

---

[23] Note that The King in Yellow is a character created by Robert Chambers in his collection of short stories by the same name. Lovecraft adopted the character in his own work, as have many other weird fiction authors.

[24] Chambers, Robert W. *The King in Yellow*. New York, NY: Fall River Press, 2014. Contains the full text of Robert W. Chambers's stories as well as an introduction and notes by S. T. Joshi. Originally published 1895.

[25] *True Detective*. "Form and Void." Episode 8. Directed by Cary Joji Fukunaga. Written by Nic Pizzolatto. HBO. March 9, 2014.

[26] Ibid.

It was for my initiation into the Anti-Brotherhood.... I had to prove I was beyond compassion. Beyond humanity... I had no compassion... no compassion... urrrrrrrrhhhhh...[27]

— Sir Miles Delacourt

Most of us understandably balk at the idea that there could be anything transcendent about the willful taking of another life, but sacrifice has long been part of religious ritual the world over. It is precisely because murder is an enormous transgression that it carries such a powerful charge for *True Detective*'s antagonist, Errol Childress. Like Sir Miles, or William Gull in *From Hell*, Childress uses his crimes to connect to the reality behind the everyday, a world, as in *The Invisibles*, where time and space fuse and may be navigated, and into which both murderer and victim are transported. Why does he sacrifice lives to the Yellow King? Because Childress feels he is a messenger enacting ultimate reality's will on Earth, and because for the children he kills, he is a torn veil opening a way into the post-human. Just as in *The King in Yellow* and the comic, you can't look at his true face without losing your mind. The domain of the spaghetti monsters, eternity itself, is ultimately beyond our capacity to symbolize: the invisible.

All your life – all your love, all your hate, all your memory, all your pain – it was all the same thing. It was all the same dream. A dream that you had inside a locked room. That dream about being.... a person. And like a lot of dreams, there's a monster at the end of it.[28]

— Rust Cohle

In *True Detective*, it's never clear what Carcosa is. We know it's a place, a network of tunnels kitted out with skulls and weird sculptures in a psychopath's back garden, but there's another Carcosa too, the one Ledoux mutters about shortly before having his mind blown out, a monster's web in which Rust and Marty are caught. Only maybe it's more than this. Perhaps - and given the parallels between the dream Rust describes above and Carcosa the actual geographical space, perhaps Carcosa is symbolic of our lives: a murky maze of pain, confusion, and death.

[27] Morrison, Grant and various artists. *The Invisibles Omnibus*. New York, NY: DC Comics, 2012.
[28] *True Detective*. "The Locked Room." Episode 3. Directed by Cary Joji Fukunaga. Written by Nic Pizzolatto. HBO. January 26, 2014.

It is in this final sense that Childress can be most readily understood as the hand of the Yellow King, a monster who stands outside this maze. He owns the maze and his voice can be heard emanating from no particular direction but everywhere inside it. Almost as though he, like the spaghetti monsters of *The Invisibles*, can intersect with it from anywhere, from 'above.' If we follow Rust's analogy to its conclusion, then the monster, Childress, is ourselves shorn of personhood. He's the brute and bloody reality Sir Miles knows is always immanent and whose presence Rust, too, must find a way to live with. As it turns out, however, he's something else, something far more benevolent.

> All of us meet the forgotten, each to his kind... When fear is all there is, there is no fear. Eternal pain is no longer pain. When we remember them recognize them for what they are, they no longer enslave us.[29]
> — John-A-Dreams

> This is your voice echoing off the walls of God.[30]
> — Elfayed

It's no coincidence that the final confrontation at Carcosa's heart involves so much rupturing and piercing. *True Detective* is often faulted for being a very macho show, a criticism I've found myself nodding along with, but the violence isn't just physical in nature but spiritual. When read in this way the violence takes on another far more positive connotation. Both *True Detective* and *The Invisibles* arrive at the same diagnosis for the protagonists' pain - alienation. Rust and Miles might have peeked behind the veil, but neither of them have really incorporated this understanding or its implications into their lives. Miles' response is classically Nietzschean, he sides with darkness and makes up his mind to be king of the shit heap, Rust just gets lost in a sea of dead children and failed relationships, but in the end, both are wallowing in their own disillusionment. They know intellectually that everything's part of the same thing. The problem is they see that thing as fundamentally grotesque and so recoil from it. They don't have the courage to approach, to make friends with the spaghetti monster, and see where that takes them.

---

[29] Morrison, Grant and various artists. *The Invisibles Omnibus*. New York, NY: DC Comics, 2012.
[30] Ibid.

I don't want to spoil the comic, so I won't tell you what happens to Miles, but by the end of *True Detective*, Rust is effectively broken open. It's as though the whole world comes rushing in through his wounds, the oneness and unity he's so horrified by suddenly becoming vivid reality. It's scary, but only at first. After crossing over into the timeless zones where everything is one and nothing ever dies, he's permitted a final goodbye to both his father and his daughter - and later, when he returns to the quotidian, that rarest of jewels in the life of Rust Cohle: a friend. It doesn't matter if any of this is 'real.' In dying, Rust finally comes to terms with the darkness and finds his loved ones - *the capacity to love* - waiting there. Where else?

The "locked room" referenced in Rust's quote above could stand in for the universe or our own heads. It doesn't matter, the point the series wants to make is we're all in this together, we're all suffering together. In a world of suffering where God is absent and only we create meaning, then imagination and compassion are perhaps more appropriate and useful responses than despair or rage. It is only by employing these tools, the ones which connect us to other people and things, the show argues, that we stand a chance of transcending.

> And when the Archons come and it all turns inside out with scary miracles. It's only all the things you left out when you were building your little house called "Me," ey?[31]
> — Jack Frost

This breaking open - or breaking *out* - occurs before the curtain falls on *The Invisibles* too, when humanity is absorbed into the fifth dimension, or as it's nicknamed in the comic, the Supercontext. What I find compelling about the comic's final act, even now that I'm less enamored with some of its more mystical pretensions, is the idea, evident at the end, that by interfacing with the Supercontext, humankind has switched places with its fifth dimensional prison wardens. That we've gone from being passive and acted upon, from being thrown into a rigid world, to becoming participants capable of truly owning ourselves and our environment. As Jack Frost, the buddha of this new age, explains:

---

[31] Ibid.

We made gods and jailers because we felt small and alone. We let them try us and sentence us and, like sheep to the slaughter, we allowed ourselves to be sentenced...[32]

What Rust is trying out at the end when he talks about the light winning is just a test run. He's tentatively taking on the responsibility of being an agent, someone unafraid to *act* and *be* in the world. Someone capable of transposing his own meanings on things, regardless of whether they contained any in the first place, instead of just giving up and sinking into the bottomless gravity well of his own personal black star, the death of his child.

The World is a veil and the face you wear is not your own."[33]
— Reverend Tuttle

The "Outer Church" you fear and the "Invisible College" you want to destroy? Same address, Sir Miles.[34]
— Helga

Inevitably, both *The Invisibles* and *True Detective* reach the same conclusion about the world we live in - that it is an annex of a wider reality where all things are one thing, *and that includes all of us*. Viewed by the fearful, this hyper-reality is terrifying, an annihilating hell presided over by yellow kings and other soul devouring monsters; but for those ready to be transformed, it becomes a gateway to a heavenly interconnectedness. Everything is a matter of perspective. Do we choose the black or the white? The light or the dark?

This interplay of perspectives, one as viable as the other, is what confirms *The Invisibles'* influence on the show. If *True Detective*'s only influences were the works of Ligotti and H.P. Lovecraft, then it would not include Rust's revelation or Reverend Theriot's sermon. Theriot's sermon is particularly interesting, as it lays bare a life affirming schematic that in no way contradicts Rust's gloomier ramblings, but instead takes a wider view. For Theriot, the unity isn't a source of horror, but a wonderful thing, where our "angers and [....]

---

[32] Ibid.

[33] *True Detective*. "The Locked Room." Episode 3. Directed by Cary Joji Fukunaga. Written by Nic Pizzolatto. HBO. January 26, 2014.

[34] Morrison, Grant and various artists. *The Invisibles Omnibus*. New York, NY: DC Comics, 2012.

griefs and [....] separations are [revealed to be a] a fevered hallucination."[35] These words resonate deeply with Rust's eventual transfiguration. It is the same transfiguration all the Invisibles, good and bad, undergo before the end.

Theriot can easily be dismissed as just another revivalist nut, his full sermon, in the show drowned out by Rust's critique, only available online. However, if we take the time to seek it out, the sermon presents us with another version of the truth no less convincing than the pessimistic take *True Detective* ostensibly endorses right up until its last scene. Isn't this where, the comic tells us, the Invisibles can only truly be found? Off the beaten track. In the alleys and the subways. In the cracks.

---

[35] *True Detective*. "The Locked Room." Episode 3. Directed by Cary Joji Fukunaga. Written by Nic Pizzolatto. HBO. January 26, 2014.

This Kind of Thing Does Not Happen in a Vacuum: The True Crime Inspiration for *True Detective*

In a 2014 interview with Entertainment Weekly, writer Nic Pizzolatto discussed some his influences for the occult themes in *True Detective*. He cited several weird fiction influences, but also hinted at a non-fiction inspiration for the crimes at the heart of the show. "Google Satanism, preschool and Louisiana," Pizzolatto suggested to his interviewer. "You'll be surprised what you get."[1] The results of Pizzolatto's suggested search are not for the faint of heart, as it leads to a very real and tragic case of child molestation which occurred at Hosanna church in Ponchatoula, Louisiana. Stuart Murphy, one of the lead detectives investigating the crimes, described it as being "the most

---

[1] Jensen, Jeff. *"True Detective* Creator Nic Pizzolatto on Carcosa, Hideous Men, and the Season 1 Endgame." Entertainment Weekly. February 27, 2014. Accessed September 24, 2018. http://www.ew.com/article/2014/02/27/true-detective-nic-pizzolatto-season-1.

bizarre case that any small-town police detective could ever imagine."[2]

In June 2005, Louis Lamonica Junior, head pastor of Hosanna church, walked into his Parish sheriff's office and confessed to crimes committed by himself and other members of his church. He listed a shocking array of crimes including bestiality, animal sacrifice, and sex with children ranging from infants to teenagers, as well as the molestation of his own children. According to Lamonica Jr., these acts were ritual satanic worship. He claimed that he and his flock regularly called forth demons and consecrated children to Satan. Lamonica Jr.'s confession remains puzzling, as it was completely unsolicited. "He didn't come to turn himself in, he came to talk with us," recalled Stan Carpenter, Parish detective supervisor. Local law enforcement acted quickly, bringing in the FBI's crimes against children unit and launching a full investigation.

Several Hosanna church members were brought in on charges,[3] but the main focus of the investigation fell on pastor Louis Lamonica Jr. and youth pastor Austin "Trey" Bernard. Interviews with Bernard, other church members, and dozens of children all corroborated the strange stories of devil worship and abuse. After searching the church's youth room, where most of the abuse occurred, and digging up the church grounds in search of buried animal carcasses, the police found no evidence of animal sacrifice or satanic rituals. Ultimately, prosecutors decided not to focus on the occult elements of the case. "The word satanic and satanic cults came up many, many times" explained Captain Stuart Murphy, "but at the end of the day it doesn't matter if they were doing what they were doing in the name of the devil or the god. They were committing a crime... against a child."[4] In 2008, Lamonica Jr. and Bernard were convicted of aggravated rape involving children. Both men are serving multiple concurrent life sentences.

---

[2] Toboni, Gianna. "The Real *True Detective*?" Vice. 2014. Accessed September 24, 2018. http://www.vice.com/video/the-real-true-detective-010. This documentary piece on the Hossana church case is well worth a watch for *True Detective* fans.

[3] One of the church members brought in on charges was Paul Fontenot. It may be coincidence that Pizzolatto used the same last name for the character Marie Fontenot, the victim whose abuse and sacrifice was captured on tape, but it could be a subtle reference to the influence of the Hossana church case.

[4] Toboni, Gianna. "The Real *True Detective*?" Vice. 2014. Accessed September 24, 2018. http://www.vice.com/video/the-real-true-detective-010.

The Real, an online documentary series by Vice, featured an excellent episode on the Hosanna church case.[5] Producer Gianna Toboni interviewed several law enforcement members who worked on the case, providing insight as to how they approached interviewing the suspects, and how they were personally impacted by disturbing details in the testimony of both the molesters and their victims. Unless otherwise noted, all quotes from Ponchatoula residents or law enforcement used in this appendix from this point forward are taken directly from interviews featured in *The Real* episode.

> My family's been here a long, long time.
> — Errol Childress

Prior to the Hosanna church scandal, Ponchatoula was known only as a footnote in Civil War history and as home to the annual Strawberry Festival, the second largest public festival in Louisiana.[6] It is a small, tight-knit community with a population hovering around 5,000 people. Long time shop owner Brenda Harris described her town as a place with history and tradition. "We have a lot of old families that have chosen to stay in this area. Families that have been here for ever and ever."

Like many communities across the South, religion is a major part of life in Ponchatoula. The town is proud of its churches and its Christian values. For many years Hosanna church was no different than any other place of worship. Under the direction of Louis Lamonica Senior, the church thrived with a membership of nearly 1,000 people. Lamonica Sr. was a local icon and a powerful preacher, but upon his death the church floundered. Eventually membership dwindled to a handful of people, led by the late pastor's son, Louis Lamonica Junior. Captain Stuart Murphy remembered the church under Lamonica Jr. as an insular group with radical beliefs. "These people were so close that it was almost their own world. Matter of fact, most of them were living there [the church building]." Though the flock was small, they were not the only people in and around the church. "There were a lot of teenage kids... that were having trouble in their own families," noted prosecutor Don Wall. "The ones that were vulnerable spent a lot of time at Louis Lamonica's house." Louis Lamonica Sr. worked hard to make his church a place of refuge for

---

[5] Ibid.
[6] The largest being Mardi Gras.

troubled kids, but detectives discovered that Lamonica Jr. soiled his father's legacy by exploiting trust in the church for his own sick purposes.

Dynastic families are a trope in Southern gothic and cosmic horror, but as the Hosanna church case demonstrates, they exist in reality as well. In *True Detective*, one branch of the proud Tuttle family slips into dissolution. Errol Childress bears a resemblance to Louis Lamonica Junior, in that both men took over their father's professions and properties, but degraded them to a point where they became twisted shadows of their original forms.

> Everybody wants confession. Everybody wants some cathartic narrative for it. The guilty especially.
> — Rust Cohle

Louis Lamonica Jr.'s confession, regardless of its motivation, was the starting point for the Hosanna church investigation. Disturbing as it was, his story was not enough to allow detectives to start issuing search warrants and rounding up possible suspects. They needed some corroboration of the abuse. For that they turned to Trey Bernard. Besides being named repeatedly in Lamonica Jr.'s confession, police felt Bernard's frequent contact with children in his role as youth pastor made him a likely suspect.

Since Bernard was not eager to confess, detectives needed to use a great deal of interrogative skill and understanding of psychology to get him talking about his role in the abuse of children. Captain Stuart Murphy explained his approach. "I don't ever play good cop/ bad cop. I don't think you get anywhere with a bad cop attitude, but you do depend on each other in a group interview to pick up on cues and weaknesses and strengths." In this case, religion was obviously the key factor. Captain Murphy and the other interviewers figured out a way to use this to their advantage with Bernard. "I can't quote scripture," Captain Murphy admitted, "but I can tell you that God will make you feel a little bit better if you confess your sins. And I did tell him that. You got to reach that level with them and the way we did that was with a little prayer... a little holding of the hands." In an amazing display of empathy and determination, the investigators sat in a small room with a man they believed had molested dozens of children and prayed with him.

Captain Murphy described the need to put emotion and judgment aside to focus on the goal of getting a confession. "When you're in that room, you've got to be even keeled, understanding. That's how we were with Trey Bernard... I was going to help him feel better about the things he did. He just needed to tell me about them." Ultimately, the strategy worked. Bernard's confession shared enough matching information with Lamonica Jr.'s to merit further investigation.

There is no interrogation scene where Detectives Hart and Cohle elicit a confession from Errol Childress, but the show does feature several interrogation scenes with other criminals and highlights Cohle's interrogation skills. Like the real-life Captain Murphy, Cohle's approach focused on putting aside judgment of the criminals who sat across the table from him. He gave them outs, excuses, and ways to minimize their roles in even the most heinous of crimes. In the scene where Cohle interrogates the "Marshland Medea,"[7] a woman accused of killing her own infant children, Cohle manages to find common ground with the woman. He admits that he lost a child as well, reaching out to hold her hand and connecting with the woman as another parent who knows the grief of losing a child. Cohle offers her S.I.D.S (Sudden Infant Death Syndrome) and Munchausen by Proxy Syndrome as ways to reduce and explain her actions, allowing her to confess to the crimes. By the time she is writing her confession, Cohle is sitting next to the woman with his arm around her, physically supporting her while she records the details of infanticide.

> Take off your mask!
> — Errol Childress

The most striking element of the Hosanna church case was how little was known about the abuse or the satanic rituals before Louis Lamonica Jr. chose to inform to the police. It was as if an evil force had been hiding in plain sight, unnoticed by the rest of town. Captain Stuart Murphy experienced this sense of unmasking when he interviewed the church's youth pastor. "When I first met Trey Bernard, he seemed to be a clean-cut, fairly intelligent guy. As I began to interview him I began to see a different side of Trey... something different than a person would normally expect. I think he's a master manipulator and a sick, sick person."

The stories told by Lamonica Jr. and Bernard seemed too strange to be true, more like fevered nightmares than anything that could possibly happen in a small town. Both men described calling forth demons as matter-of-factly as they discussed where they lived and worked. They claimed to have sacrificed

---

[7] *True Detective*. "Haunted Houses." Episode 6. Directed by Cary Joji Fukunaga. Written by Nic Pizzolatto. HBO. February 23, 2014.

dogs and cats, drinking blood and using it to draw pentagrams on the carpet of the church youth room. Lamonica Jr. believed that he experienced physical transformations when demons entered his body and that he was in animal form when having sex with children "... sometimes it would be like a snake, like a fox, wolf spiders." He told the police, "My face would distort." This sort of fantastical thinking among the Hosanna flock made it difficult for detectives to separate truth from fiction. Captain Murphy explained. "The culture of that church at that time, they believed in talking and confessing to each other these sins. They would gather around and talk about the horrible things they'd done to children in front of each other and in front of the children."

Investigators met with dozens of children named in the confessions of Lamonica Jr. and Bernard, but only two children gave detailed accounts of abuse - Lamonica Jr.'s sons. Aged 15 and 18 at the time of the investigation, the boys testified that their father began molesting them from their earliest memories. Along with their verbal accounts, the boys made disturbingly graphic drawings[8] detailing the abused they suffered. The drawings were submitted to the court as evidence along with the children's verbal accounts of their abuse.

Drawings from the younger Lamonica boy featured what appear to be hybrid half-human, half-animal creatures engaging in sexual acts. This detail is echoed in *True Detective* when Cohle tracks down Johnny Joanie, a genderqueer prostitute and former student of Tuttle's Wellspring schools. Reluctant to discuss the abuse, Johnny insists that what happened to him was so strange that no one would believe him. "There were men. Taking pictures. Sometimes... other things. They had animal faces. That's why I decided it had to be a dream."[9] In both the Hosanna church case and *True Detective*, adults manufactured unbelievable fictions, using them to confuse children and mask the truth if any child dared come forward to report the abuse.

---

[8] In *True Detective* episode 2, "Seeing Things," Marty Hart and his wife discover crude sexual drawings made by their daughter Maggie. These drawings do not come up again, but several fan theories see them as evidence that Audrey was molested by members of the Yellow King cult.

[9] *True Detective*. "After You've Gone." Episode 7. Directed by Cary Joji Fukunaga. Written by Nic Pizzolatto. HBO. March 2, 2014.

We didn't get 'em all.
— Rust Cohle

Though they were able to convict Louis Lamonica Jr. and Trey Bernard, some of the investigators in the Hosanna church case feel that they did not catch all of the abusers or get full justice for the victims. "The scary thing is we only learned so much... and we can only prosecute on what we learn." Captain Murphy said, "I think it went way, way deeper than what the prosecutor was able to bring in. I'd be a fool to sit here and think that we found out everything that happened in that church. What's scary is to think what we didn't find out..." Years later, after the case was closed and Hosanna church building abandoned, prosecutor Don Wall tried to bring in some of children named in the case, thinking that since they were safe from their abusers, the kids (now teens and young adults) would share more information. He was unable to get any of the teens to talk. After their father was sentenced to life in prison, Lamonica Jr.'s sons attempted to retract their testimonies and denied that any abuse had taken place.

Like the Hosanna church case, the investigation at the heart of *True Detective* does not come to a full resolution. At the end of the story Errol Childress, Reggie Ledoux, and Dewall Ledoux are all dead, but over the course of the investigation it became clear to Detectives Hart and Cohle that the men they stopped were smaller pieces in a much larger puzzle. Ultimately the detectives learn that the systematic abuse of children and exploitation of vulnerable populations will continue as long as the Tuttle family holds power in Louisiana. Somehow, Detectives Hart and Cohle must make peace with this, knowing that they did what they could to stop the evil they uncovered. Captain Stuart Murphy described this frustration in his characteristically straightforward manner. "What I don't like about being a detective is you never get a sense of accomplishment... there's always more stuff to do tomorrow."

Just the Facts, Ma'am: Controversy Regarding the Influence of Thomas Ligotti's Work in *True Detective*

Of the numerous works writer Nic Pizzolatto has cited as influences on *True Detective*, one book garnered the most discussion: *The Conspiracy Against the Human Race: A Contrivance of Horror* (hereafter *Conspiracy*). Written by American horror author Thomas Ligotti, the book is a non-fiction treatise on pessimist philosophy as applied to horror fiction and the horrors of everyday life.[1] Ligotti is better known for his short fiction, the themes of which permeate the atmosphere of the first half of *True Detective*. Putting aside the contraversy, fans of *True Detective* absolutely should be reading Thomas Ligotti. Nebula and Shirley Jackson Award winning author Jeff VanderMeer provides a helpful introduction to Ligotti's work and suggestions for first time readers in a 2014 article for Vulture entitled, "Thomas Ligotti 101: A Guide to the Cult Writer Now

---

[1] For an overview of *Conspiracy Against the Human Race*, see: Thacker, Eugene. "We Do Not Belong Here." Mute. March 19, 2003. Accessed September 20, 2018. http://www.metamute.org/editorial/occultural-studies-column/we-are-not-here.

Linked to *True Detective*."[2]

Astute fans and critics noticed similarities between Rust Cohle's world view and Ligotti's writing in *Conspiracy* soon after the first episode aired. Interest turned to controversy when some fans made allegations that Pizzolatto plagiarized *Conspiracy*, relying on Ligotti's words to form the backbone of Rust Cohle's darkly poetic voice and philosophical ramblings. The allegations stirred passionate response from fans of *True Detective*, fans of Ligotti, and arts and entertainment critics. In this maelstrom of opinion and outrage, some of the less inflammatory yet more salient points of the story have been overlooked. The following chapter endeavors to return focus to the facts of the story, to provide a timeline of key interviews, accusations, evidence and rebuttals. It also aims to clarify the difference between plagiarism as an ethical concept as opposed to a legal concept, and who holds the final word on whether or not an author's work has been used inappropriately.[3]

The Legal Definition of Plagiarism (or Lack Thereof)

Plagiarism is commonly understood as the theft of a recognizable set of words, sounds, or images from a published or otherwise publicly displayed original work. The key idea being that the plagiarist copies the work of another individual and passes it off as his own without crediting the original creator. Though the definition of plagiarism exists in several legal dictionaries, the charge of "plagiarism" does not exist in any civil or criminal statute. "For an act to be criminal and punishable by law legislation would need to be passed by either a state legislature or the U.S. Congress. As a matter of federal law... there is no national crime of plagiarism... there is criminal liability for certain

---

[2] VanderMeer, Jeff. "Thomas Ligotti 101: A Guide to the Cult Writer Now Linked to *True Detective*." Vulture. August 13, 2014. Accessed September 22, 2018. http://www.vulture.com/2014/08/thomas-ligotti-true-detective-guide.html#.

[3] Disclaimer: the author is not a lawyer and discusses plagiarism and copyright infringement in broad strokes so that the reader may differentiate between the two concepts. Any readers seeking more detailed information about plagiarism, copyright, and intellectual property in multiple media formats (e.g. from print to film or television) can visit the Digital Media Law Project (http://www.dmlp.org/) which provides in-depth discussion of rights in plain language for authors and publishers.

copyright infringement."[4] Stuart P. Green, Professor of Law at Rutgers School of Law, notes that plagiarism, "is not, strictly speaking, a legal concept," and thus, "it has mostly been ignored by legal commentators."[5]

Outside of a court of law, plagiarism is considered a moral or ethical violation and can result in career-ending repercussions. In the fields of academia and journalism, there are codes of conduct and guidelines about what does and does not constitute plagiarism. In the sphere of literature, arts and entertainment, however, there are no clear guidelines. The problem lies in the fact that any work of fiction is, to some extent, influenced by the stories and artwork that preceded it. Drawing a line between influence, homage, allusion, satire, pastiche, and plagiarism is difficult and highly subjective. As Jonathan Lethem notes in an essay for Harper's Magazine, "finding one's voice isn't just an emptying and purifying oneself of the words of others but an adopting and embracing of filiations, communities, and discourses... Invention, it must be humbly admitted, does not consist in creating out of void but out of chaos."[6] Fiction, as Rust Cohle would say, "does not happen in a vacuum."[7]

The Parties Involved

There are three main parties involved in the *True Detective* plagiarism controversy. The first party is composed of Nic Pizzolatto, the writer/ creator of *True Detective* and HBO, the cable network which airs the program. Pizzolatto was born and educated in Louisiana. Prior to his work with television, he published novels and short fiction, and held teaching positions at the University of North Carolina at Chapel Hill, the University of Chicago, and DePauw University. His television work before *True Detective* was limited to writing two episodes for *The Killing*, another crime drama series. Along with being the sole

---

[4] Richman, Steven M. *What You Need to Know About Plagiarism*. New Jersey State Bar Foundation. 2016. Accessed September 20, 2018. https://njsbf.org.

[5] Green, Stuart P. "Plagiarism, Norms, and the Limits of Theft Law: Some Observations on the Use of Criminal Sanctions in Enforcing Intellectual Property Rights." *SSRN Electronic Journal* 54 (2002). Accessed September 21, 2018. doi:10.2139/ssrn.315562.

[6] Lethem, Jonathan. "The Ecstasy of Influence: A Plagiarism." *Harper's Magazine*, February 1, 2007, 57-71. Available in Harper's online archives at: http://harpers.org/archive/2007/02/

[7] *True Detective*. "The Long Bright Dark." Episode 1. Directed by Cary Joji Fukunaga. Written by Nic Pizzolatto. HBO. January 12, 2014.

writer for *True Detective*, Pizzolatto also served as executive producer and show runner.

The second party is composed of horror author Thomas Ligotti and Hippocampus Press, the publisher of *Conspiracy*. Ligotti began publishing in the 1980s and since then has penned several collections of award winning short stories, poems, and screenplays. Described by *The Washington Post* as the best kept secret in contemporary horror fiction, Ligotti has a passionate fan base in the horror and weird fiction communities. His lack of a presence at literary events and on social media contributes to Ligotti's reputation as a recluse.[8] *Conspiracy* is Ligotti's first non-fiction work. Although he discusses nihilist, anti-natalist, and pessimist philosophy at length, Thomas Ligotti is not a philosopher. In a 2006 interview with Ligotti, Matt Cardin noted, "Ligotti has identified himself as a horror writer. He doesn't want to be known as anything else. He has, on occasion, taken exception when people have tried to label him otherwise."[9]

The third party is composed of Jon Padgett, founder of Thomas Ligotti Online (TLO) and Mike Davis, editor of The Lovecraft eZine. In an online author biography, Padgett describes himself as "...the first publisher for a number of Ligotti's prose works, including *My Work is Not Yet Done* and *Crampton*."[10] Although Padgett is in contact with Ligotti, a disclaimer on the Thomas Ligotti Online site makes it clear he does not speak for the author. The disclaimer reads, "It is important to note that while all copyright-related content is presented with the permission of Thomas Ligotti, TLO was created upon the solitary actions of Jon Padgett and continues to exist independent of the

---

[8] Anxiety has been a factor in Ligotti's reclusiveness, however anxiety disorders are not the only reason for a writer to shy away from public life. When one considers the number of journalists, critics, bloggers, and fans looking to profit from controversy (real or manufactured), perhaps retiring from the media spotlight is the most sensible option for a creator.

[9] Cardin, Matt. "It's a Matter of Personal Pathology: An Interview with Thomas Ligotti." *The New York Review of Science Fiction* #218, October 2006, 1-7. Free transcript of interview available at http://www.teemingbrain.com/interview-with-thomas-ligotti/.

[10] "Jon Padgett (Author of *The Secret of Ventriloquism*)." Goodreads. Accessed September 22, 2018. https://www.goodreads.com/author/show/7189686.Jon_Padgett.

direction or promotion of Thomas Ligotti."[11] Similarly, Mike Davis's site, The Lovecraft eZine, does not appear to be formally affiliated with the Lovecraft literary estate. Both Padgett and Davis have dedicated themselves to creating fertile online fan communities and promoting weird fiction.

The Timeline of Allegations

True Detective premiered on HBO on January 12th, 2014 and was an immediate hit, becoming the most watched freshman show in the network's history.[12] Though the first season contained only eight episodes, critics and fans alike began analyzing the dense web of literary and philosophical allusions well before the finale aired in March 2014. Adding to the excitement, writer Nic Pizzolatto gave several interviews while the show was on the air, discussing the influences behind the popular series.

On January 21st, The Arkham Digest published an interview with Pizzolatto, asking him about "Cohle's Ligottian worldview."[13] The interviewer's question was multi-part and also mentioned the cryptic stick sculptures which appear in the show and a possible connection to Karl Edward Wagner's story "Sticks." Pizzolatto included several horror writers as influences in his answer to the reviewer's question, but made no mention of Thomas Ligotti. The Arkham Digest interview made no accusations of plagiarism or improper use of Ligotti's material, but in the comments section of the article, an anonymous user's question foreshadowed the controversy to come. "Is it just me," the anonymous commenter asked, "or is Pizzolatto being coy about the obvious Ligotti influence?"[14]

On January 30th, Michael Calia wrote an article for the Wall Street Journal Online detailing the influence of Ligotti's *Conspiracy* on Cohle's worldview and

---

[11] "TLO Statement." Thomas Ligotti Online. Accessed September 22, 2018. http://www.ligotti.net/view.php?pg=info_aboutus.

[12] Andreeva, Nellie. "*True Detective* Now Most Watched HBO Freshman Series Ever." Deadline. April 15, 2014. Accessed September 22, 2018. http://www.deadline.com/2014/04/true-detective-now-most-watched-hbo-freshman-series-ever/.

[13] Steele, Justin. "Interview: Nic Pizzolatto, Creator/ Writer of HBO's *True Detective*." The Arkham Digest. January 21, 2014. Accessed September 22, 2018. http://www.arkhamdigest.com/2014/01/interview-nic-pizzolatto-creatorwriter.html.

[14] Ibid.

dialogue in *True Detective*. In the interview, Calia made no accusations of plagiarism or improper use of Ligotti's material, but did provide a few side-by-side comparisons between Cohle's dialogue and passages from *Conspiracy*.

The comments section of the Wall Street Journal Online article quickly filled with reader feedback. As with most online discourse, comments on the article were anonymous, but one commentator raised questions about the extent of Pizzolatto's use of Ligotti's work. The commentator used the screen name "Dr. Locrian."[15] This user's first comment on the article[16] lists many of the same passages from *Conspiracy* that John Padgett and Mike Davis would later cite in their August 4th accusation of plagiarism. In the article comments, user Dr. Locrian states that Pizzolatto "... has been obtrusively silent about Ligotti -- even when asked directly about him"[17] (presumably referencing the January 21st interview with Arkham Digest). Dr. Locrian went on to say, "I'm not drawing any conclusions or making any judgments yet about plagiarism. Maybe there will be a big Ligotti reveal later in the show. Or he's waiting till everything is said and done to mention him. Who knows?"[18]

Later in the day on January 30th, The Arkham Digest published a follow-up interview with Pizzolatto specifically to address the influence of Thomas Ligotti's work on *True Detective*. Interviewer Justin Steele asked Pizzolatto, "Some readers seem surprised that you didn't mention Ligotti as a direct influence on Cohle, and some were of the opinion you were simply being coy about it... How influential has his writing been on not only Cohle, but on the

---

[15] Comments by user "Dr. Locrian" are included in this article to represent the general content and tone of the online discussions around Pizzolatto's alleged misuse of Ligotti's work. A person with the username "Dr. Locrian" commented on several of the key articles about Pizzolatto and Ligotti, making "Dr. Locrian" a convenient stand-in for the many voices involved in the online debate. User "Dr. Locrian" is anonymous and his or her identity is unknown to the author.

[16] Calia, Michael. "The Most Shocking Thing About HBO's *True Detective*." The Wall Street Journal. January 30, 2014. Accessed September 22, 2018. http://blogs.wsj.com/speakeasy/2014/01/30/the-most-shocking-thing-about-hbos-true-detective/tab/comments/. First comment time stamped at 12:47 pm January 30, 2014

[17] Ibid.

[18] Ibid.

series as a whole?"[19]

Pizzolatto's answer was unequivocal. "The work and vision of Thomas Ligotti was very influential for imagining Cohle's overall worldview."[20] Pizzolatto's complete answer emphasized the connection between his work and that of several other authors, stating "there was a clear line to me from Chambers to Lovecraft to Ligotti, and their fictional visions of cosmic despair were articulating the same things as certain nihilist and pessimist philosophers, but with more poetry and art and vision."[21] Pizzolatto also indicated that he had hoped to hold off on discussing the philosophical influences on the show until after the final episode. "I suppose I've been overly wary of having people define Cohle solely based on the philosophy he espouses in the first three episodes, because the truth is that the whole of his character and his journey is much more complex than that." Pizzolatto went on to add, "if this leads people to discover and explore Ligotti's work, then I'll be very happy."[22]

On February 2nd, Pizzolatto did another interview with Michael Calia for the Wall Street Journal Online, again focusing on the Ligotti influence on *True Detective*. When asked to name a single work of weird fiction and/or horror he would recommend, Pizzolatto named several authors, including Ligotti. "I'd point people in the direction of Thomas Ligotti, Laird Barron, John Langan, Simon Strantzas and others."[23] When asked specifically about Ligotti's influence on his own work, Pizzolatto said, "I read *The Conspiracy Against the Human Race* and found it incredibly powerful writing,"[24] explaining that Cohle's monologue on pessimism early in the show was a deliberate homage to Ligotti. "In episode one, there are two lines in particular (and it would have been nothing to re-word them) that were specifically phrased in such a way as to

---

[19] Steele, Justin. "*True Detective*'s Nic Pizzolatto on Ligotti." The Arkham Digest. January 30, 2014. Accessed September 22, 2018. http://www.arkhamdigest.com/2014/01/true-detectives-nic-pizzolatto-on.html.

[20] Ibid.

[21] Ibid.

[22] Ibid.

[23] Calia, Michael. "Writer Nic Pizzolatto on Thomas Ligotti and the Weird Secrets of *True Detective*." The Wall Street Journal. February 02, 2014. Accessed September 22, 2018. http://blogs.wsj.com/speakeasy/2014/02/02/writer-nic-pizzolatto-on-thomas-ligotti-and-the-weird-secrets-of-true-detective/.

[24] Ibid.

signal Ligotti admirers."[25] Calia made no mention of plagiarism accusations in the interview.

At the time of the February 2nd interview with the Wall Street Journal Online, only three episodes of *True Detective* had aired. In the interview, Pizzolatto repeated the concern that his commentary could negatively impact the viewer's experience of the show, saying, "I've put off going into the philosophy Cohle espouses in the early episodes because I don't want people making assumptions about the character of Cohle, or the ultimate aim of this season... The totality of Cohle's character and the show's agenda won't be clear until the eighth episode has ended."[26]

The final episode of the first season of *True Detective* aired in March of 2014. By August 2014, the first season of *True Detective* had been over for four months. The show generated countless think pieces dissecting every aspect of the work, including Pizzolatto's literary and film influences. Interest in the show still ran high, but by late summer, Ligotti's influence on Pizzolatto and *True Detective* was no longer breaking news.

On August 4th, 2014 Jon Padgett and Mike Davis published an accusation that Pizzolatto was guilty of misappropriating Ligotti's work. Padgett and Davis published their thoughts on *True Detective* on the Lovecraft eZine website in an interview-style post titled "Did the Writer of *True Detective* Plagiarize Thomas Ligotti and Others?"[27] The title is phrased as a question, but the body of the post made it clear that Padgett and Davis had no doubt about the matter. Davis, as editor of the Lovecraft eZine, noted in his introduction that he was not conducting the interview from a neutral standpoint. Davis shared Padgett's concerns about plagiarism stating, "I have agonized over whether I should write this article, in the end I felt that morally I have no choice."[28]

The article cites eight lines of Rust Cohle's dialogue from *True Detective* as proof of the plagiarism, making a side-by-side comparison with nineteen lines from Ligotti's *Conspiracy*. In the article, Davis uses a quote from the University

---

[25] Ibid.

[26] Ibid.

[27] Davis, Mike. "Did the Writer of *True Detective* Plagiarize Thomas Ligotti and Others?" Lovecraft EZine. August 04, 2014. Accessed September 22, 2018. http://lovecraftzine.com/2014/08/04/did-the-writer-of-true-detective-plagiarize-thomas-ligotti-and-others/.

[28] Ibid.

of Cambridge's policy on plagiarism as their definition of plagiarism; however, he fails to note that the definition is purely for academic purposes and is only binding for students of the University of Cambridge. Additionally, he cites the fact that Ligotti is not mentioned in any of the extras available on the *True Detective* Blu-Ray box set as evidence that Pizzolatto was attempting to obscure the influence of Ligotti's work, despite the fact that serialized fiction in the television broadcast format does not have established conventions for rigorous, academic style citations. The television broadcast format does not lend itself to footnotes or in-text citations in the same way as a printed work. Some writers and creators provide interviews and information about source material in DVD commentaries or extras, but others do not.

In his introduction to the interview, Davis acknowledges that Pizzolatto spoke about Ligotti's influence on his work in the Arkham Digest and the Wall Street Journal Online interviews, but claims that Pizzolatto discusses Ligotti only "when he is directly asked about him — in other words, when he has no choice."[29] Padgett goes on to dismiss the idea that Pizzolatto's use of Ligotti was homage. "'Homage' suggests that Pizzolatto was honoring Ligotti or showing him respect of some sort. Lifting Ligotti's work without permission or attribution may have or may not have been a consciously malicious decision, but in any case it was neither honorable nor reverential."[30] Note that by including the phrase, "without attribution" Padgett and Davis contradict their earlier acknowledgement that Pizzolatto did, in fact, cite Ligotti in both his Arkham Digest and Wall Street Journal Online interviews. Pizzolatto listed Ligotti as a direct influence for not just the ideas, but also the wording of key lines of dialogue in *True Detective*.

Padgett ends the piece by appealing directly to Emmy Award voters, saying, "I'd like the Emmy voters to know that, though Pizzolatto has made a big deal of being the show's creator and sole writer, everything special about *True Detective*'s writing was arguably written (word for word or paraphrased) by others... In my opinion, he doesn't deserve to be nominated for the Outstanding Writing Emmy award, let alone be the recipient of such an award."[31]

---

[29] Ibid.
[30] Ibid.
[31] Ibid.

The Evidence

When examining the eight lines of dialogue submitted by Padgett and Davis as evidence of Pizzolatto's plagiarism of Ligotti, it is important to remember that *Conspiracy* is a review and analysis of a large body of philosophy and literature. In his book, Ligotti references the works of dozens of philosophers and writers.[32] When not quoting them directly, Ligotti summarizes, rephrases, or expands upon the ideas of other writers and philosophers. Ligotti's extensive research and detailed analysis of the existing body of pessimist thought is an admirable achievement. He makes careful selections from texts that can be extremely dry and dense, highlighting their sinister implications with a clarity that makes their logic compelling. Ligotti presents his own original ideas in the book as well, adding them to the existing body of pessimist thought. This is where the fact that Thomas Ligotti is an author and not a philosopher becomes vital. It's a small distinction, but an important one, as many who cry plagiarism forget that much of what they read in *Conspiracy* does not originate with Ligotti -- only his summaries, analysis and application of the philosophies are unique. Ligotti uses citations and extensive notes to give proper attribution for his source material. Commentators on Ligotti's work and/or its influence on *True Detective* have a definitive resource to differentiate between Ligotti's words and those belonging to the authors he cites. To suggest that Ligotti is responsible for the whole body of philosophical thought included in *Conspiracy* is to erase the contributions of the original authors and philosophers.

Given that so much of Ligotti's work in *Conspiracy* is intrinsically tied to the ideas of other authors and philosophers, claims that Pizzolatto plagiarized the work cannot be based on the fact that Pizzolatto used the same philosophical source material as Ligotti. That philosophical and literary source material does not belong to Ligotti, nor is he the only person with rights to use it as inspiration; it belongs to the original authors and any writer is free to use it for inspiration. Therefore, any claims of plagiarism must be based on Pizzolatto's use of Ligotti's exact, original wording as it appears in the text of *Conspiracy*.

---

[32] Ligotti quotes from and discusses the works of: H.P. Lovecraft, Algernon Blackwood, Julius Bahnsen, William James, Friedrich Nietzsche, Arthur Schopenhauer, Peter Wessel Zapffe, Thomas Metzinger, Nicholas Humphrey, Philipp Mainländer, Carlo Michelstaedter, Émile Coué, Miguel de Unamuno, David Benetar, Blaise Pascal, Joshua Foa Dienstag, and many others.

In their comparison of the eight lines of *True Detective* dialogue against the 248 pages of *Conspiracy,* Padgett and Davis are rarely able to find an extended run of matching words between two texts. One of their examples, culled from Cohle's dialogue in the premier episode (strings of exactly matching words in bold text):

> We are things that labor under the illusion of having a 'self'...each of us programmed with total assurance that we're each somebody, when in fact **everybody is nobody**."[33]

This one line cannot be matched to a single line of Ligotti's text. Instead, Padgett and Davis must cobble together four separate quotes from *Conspiracy* to form a rough approximation of the *True Detective* line. The four quotes are not closely grouped in the original text – they appear peppered over approximately 90 pages in Ligotti's book. Additionally, the longest string of exactly matching words appearing in the example is only three words long: "everybody is nobody." The other strings of words in the Ligotti examples are similar, but not an exact match for the *True Detective* line. The quotes Padgett and Davis cite as proof the above line from *True Detective* constitutes theft are:

> And the worst possible thing we could know — worse than knowing of our descent from a mass of microorganisms — is that we are nobodies not somebodies, puppets not people. (*Conspiracy*, p. 109)
>
> **Everybody is nobody**... (*Conspiracy*, p. 199)
>
> ...our captivity in the illusion of a self – even though "there is no one" to have this illusion... (*Conspiracy*, p. 107)
>
> ...the illusion of being a somebody among somebodies as well as for the substance we see, or think we see, in the world... (*Conspiracy*, p. 114)

Of the eight examples of *True Detective* dialogue analyzed by Padgett and Davis, one example might fit the criteria of being an extended word-for-word match. The line is drawn from Cohle's first episode dialogue about pessimist philosophy (again, strings of exactly matching words are in bold text):

> We became too self-aware. Nature created an aspect of nature separate from itself. We are creatures that **should not exist by natural law**.[34]

The matching line from Ligotti reads:

> We know that nature has veered into the supernatural by fabricating a creature that cannot and **should not exist by natural law**, and yet does. (*Conspiracy*, p.111)

---

[33] *True Detective.* "The Long Bright Dark." Episode 1. Directed by Cary Joji Fukunaga. Written by Nic Pizzolatto. HBO. January 12, 2014.
[34] Ibid.

In this example the exact string of words that is the same in both *True Detective* and *Conspiracy* is six words long: "should not exist by natural law." These few, short matching word strings are the strongest textual evidence that Pizzolatto plagiarized Ligotti's words exactly as they appear in *Conspiracy*.

Padgett and Davis's examples falter as hard evidence of word-for-word plagiarism, but they do succeed in illustrating that Pizzolatto's writing in *True Detective* draws heavily on the same philosophical ideas explored by Ligotti and echoes the general tone of his writing. The pessimist, nihilist, and anti-natalist philosophy Ligotti reviews in *Conspiracy* forms the backbone of Rust Cohle's character and personal conflict over the course of the show. Rust Cohle is the flagship character of *True Detective* and it is his existential angst that elevates the show to a more literary level of storytelling not often seen on television. In that sense, the success of *True Detective* owes a great deal to Thomas Ligotti as well as all of the philosophers and authors Ligotti included in *Conspiracy*.

The Response

As soon as Davis and Padgett published the blog post accusing Pizzolatto of plagiarism, the comments section of The Lovecraft eZine lit up. The debate soon spread to social media and traditional media outlets. HBO and Pizzolatto made no immediate response to the accusations, but the attention the post garnered spurred Mike Davis to write a follow up on August 5th, one day after the original posting. In it he clarified that although the first post mentioned other recent cases of plagiarism which resulted in legal action, he was not suggesting that the evidence he and Padgett presented would stand up in a court of law. He also claimed any readers focused on the legality of Pizzolatto's use of Ligotti's work were "missing the point," and that "Nic Pizzolatto may or may not have done anything illegal. But what he did was certainly wrong. He went too far."[35] Davis further emphasized that he did not accept Pizzolatto's mentions of Ligotti in the Arkham Digest and Wall Street Journal Online interviews as sincere or sufficient acknowledgement for the debt *True Detective* owes to Ligotti's work. He explained his decision to write the original post was a way of championing author's rights. Posing the question "…if we allow Nic Pizzolatto to get away

---

[35] Davis, Mike. "Nic Pizzolatto's 'Homage' to Ligotti: Right and Wrong vs. the Law and the Courts." Lovecraft EZine. August 05, 2014. Accessed September 22, 2018. http://lovecraftzine.com/2014/08/05/nic-pizzolattos-homage-to-ligotti-right-and-wrong-vs-the-law-and-the-courts/.

with pawning off those key Cohle statements as his own, then where does it end?"[36] Davis's argument ignores the fact that Pizzolatto *did* acknowledge Ligotti's influence in at least two separate interviews and that Pizzolatto admitted that "there are two lines in particular (and it would have been nothing to re-word them) that were specifically phrased in such a way as to signal Ligotti admirers."[37] The fact that Davis did not approve of the acknowledgements or their timing does not erase the fact that they did, indeed, happen.

On August 7th, 2014 HBO and Nic Pizzolatto issued separate statements which firmly denied any wrongdoing and notably omitted any mention of Ligotti. The HBO statement stood by Pizzolatto:

> *True Detective* is a work of exceptional originality and the story, plot, characters and dialogue are that of Nic Pizzolatto. Philosophical concepts are free for anyone to use, including writers of fiction, and there have been many such examples in the past. Exploring and engaging with ideas and themes that philosophers and novelists have wrestled with over time is one of the show's many strengths -- we stand by the show, its writing and Nic Pizzolatto entirely.[38]

Pizzolatto's personal statement also focused on the fact that philosophical ideas are not exclusive to any one writer, saying:

> Nothing in the television show *True Detective* was plagiarized. The philosophical thoughts expressed by Rust Cohle do not represent any thought or idea unique to any one author; rather these are the philosophical tenets of a pessimistic, anti-natalist philosophy with an historic tradition including Arthur Schopenauer, Friedrich Nietzche, E.M. Cioran, and various other philosophers, all of whom express these ideas. As an autodidact pessimist, Cohle speaks toward that philosophy with erudition and in his own words. The ideas within this philosophy are certainly not exclusive to any writer.[39]

---

[36] Ibid.

[37] Calia, Michael. "Writer Nic Pizzolatto on Thomas Ligotti and the Weird Secrets of *True Detective*." The Wall Street Journal. February 02, 2014. Accessed September 22, 2018. http://blogs.wsj.com/speakeasy/2014/02/02/writer-nic-pizzolatto-on-thomas-ligotti-and-the-weird-secrets-of-true-detective/.

[38] Jagernauth, Kevin. "HBO & Nic Pizzolatto Issue Official Statements Denying Plagiarism Charge Against *True Detective*." IndieWire. August 07, 2014. Accessed September 22, 2018. http://blogs.indiewire.com/theplaylist/hbo-nic-pizzolatto-issue-official-statements-denying-plagiarism-charge-against-true-detective-20140807.

[39] Ibid.

As of the time of this book's publication, Thomas Ligotti has released no statement commenting on or acknowledging the use of his work in *True Detective*.

The Rights and Responsibilities

The fact that fiction is always influenced by other works of art and literature is not permission for authors to commit wholesale theft or misrepresentation. Authors who feel that their work has been plagiarized have legal recourse. Copyright infringement is usually the statute authors or publishers use when suing plagiarists, though it is important to note that copyright infringement is not the same thing as plagiarism; it is a violation of the rights of the copyright holder. It occurs when copyrighted material is used without the consent of the copyright holder, or when copyrighted material is used in a way which violates the terms of the license issued by the copyright holder. Most importantly, the only party with the right to sue for copyright infringement is the party which owns copyright on the work in question.

The top of the copyright page of *Conspiracy* states, "Copyright © 2010 Thomas Ligotti."[40] This notice alerts readers that the material within the book is subject to copyright and identifies the year of first publication as well as the name of the copyright owner. The second portion of the copyright notice for *Conspiracy* reads "All rights reserved. No part of this work may be reproduced in any form or by any means without the written permission of the publisher."[41] This portion of the copyright notice informs readers that Ligotti and his publisher withhold all rights to the maximum extent allowable by the law. Thomas Ligotti and Hippocampus Press are the only parties with the legal right to re-publish or reuse the text or excerpts of the text of *Conspiracy*, and they are the only ones with the right to grant usage of the text to any third party. This also means Thomas Ligotti and Hippocampus Press are the only parties with the legal right to sue for copyright infringement on the original material in *Conspiracy*.

When owners of copyrighted material feel their work has been used in a way that violates copyright, they can pursue a lawsuit against the offending

---

[40] Ligotti, Thomas. *The Conspiracy Against the Human Race: A Contrivance of Horror*. New York: Hippocampus Press, 2010.
[41] Ibid.

party to stop usage and seek compensation for damages. Alternately, the copyright holder can arbitrate a settlement that is amenable to both parties and allows the copyright holder to be compensated for the use of their work and for any damages the wrongful use may have incurred. Both the lawsuit and the settlement options involve a great deal of time, paperwork, and legal fees, but the settlement option usually provides the fastest and least painful resolution for all parties involved. Additionally, settlements can include a non-disclosure agreement as part of the terms of the settlement. Non-disclosure agreements stipulate that neither party can discuss the terms of the settlement once it has been finalized. Silence regarding the settlement can be beneficial to both the accused copyright infringer and the copyright owner, as it allows both parties to avoid negative press and minimizes damage to any pre-existing or future business relationship between the parties.

The accusers in the *True Detective* plagiarism controversy – Jon Padgett and Mike Davis – hold no copyright on Ligotti's writing in *Conspiracy*. As such, they have no legal standing to sue for copyright infringement or seek damages; they also have no rights to do so on behalf of Ligotti.

In their August 4th blog post, Padgett and Davis lament, "the sad fact is that this controversy could've been avoided had Pizzolatto reached out to Ligotti for permission to use his work in the first place."[42] In making this statement, Padgett and Davis are making a serious allegation: that Pizzolatto / HBO had *not previously* negotiated acceptable terms for the use of his copyrighted work in *True Detective*, nor were they currently (as of August 2014), negotiating acceptable terms of use. Padgett and Davis present no evidence for their assertion that Pizzolatto / HBO failed to reach out to Ligotti or his publisher. This may be because Padgett and Davis are in no way involved in Thomas Ligotti's business dealings regarding *Conspiracy*, thus they have no way to know what license or settlement, if any, exists between Ligotti and Pizzolatto / HBO. To cry plagiarism when lacking such a vital piece of evidence is a bold move.

Fans and critics do not have a legal right to make claims of plagiarism or copyright infringement on behalf of their favorite authors. They do, however,

---

[42] Davis, Mike. "Did the Writer of *True Detective* Plagiarize Thomas Ligotti and Others?" Lovecraft EZine. August 04, 2014. Accessed September 22, 2018. http://lovecraftzine.com/2014/08/04/did-the-writer-of-true-detective-plagiarize-thomas-ligotti-and-others/.

have the opportunity to educate *True Detective* viewers on the body of literature, philosophy, and film which inspired the show. Writing about the works that influenced *True Detective* does not require that the author be a fan of the show or Nic Pizzolatto. It is entirely possible to call out references, similarities, and provide in-depth analysis while simultaneously espousing the idea that the show is derivative, not in keeping with a Ligottian world view, or not worthy of industry awards. Critics and fans that hold those opinions can state their case without making accusations of plagiarism. In fact, making accusations of plagiarism can distract from important conversations about the ethics of literature, movies, and television which rely heavily on references to other, pre-existing works. It is difficult to have a rational, meaningful discourse when the conversation is predicated on the idea that one author is guilty of stealing from another. As Jonathan Bailey noted in a blog post on Plagiarism Today, "so while it's a conversation worth having, it's one best had without a lynch mob."[43]

The Impact

The first season of *True Detective* was nominated for over two dozen awards for writing, directing, performance, casting, make-up, and title design, emphasizing the overall excellence of the show's production. Though he was nominated for the award, Nic Pizzolatto did not win the Emmy for Outstanding Writing for a Drama Series. It is unclear if the accusations of plagiarism by Padgett and Davis had anything to do with that outcome, or if *Breaking Bad's* Moira Walley-Beckett was simply the stronger contender. The first season of *True Detective* did well with critics, being hailed as among the best television shows of 2014 by Metacritic,[44] and did well enough that HBO aired a second and third season of the show. Accusations of plagiarism did not appear to hamper Nic Pizzolatto's career. He won the award for Best Drama Series and

[43] Bailey, Jonathan. "*True Detective*, Less True Plagiarism." Plagiarism Today. August 26, 2014. Accessed September 22, 2018. https://www.plagiarismtoday.com/2014/08/26/true-detective-less-true-plagiarism/.

[44] Dietz, Jason. "Best of 2014: Television Critic Top Ten Lists." Metacritic. December 09, 2014. Accessed September 22, 2018. http://www.metacritic.com/feature/tv-critics-pick-10-best-tv-shows-of-2014.

Best New Series from the 67th Writers Guild of America Awards, and is the writer/creator for the second and third seasons of *True Detective*.

The controversy surrounding their claims that Pizzolatto plagiarized Ligotti increased the visibility of John Padgett's website, Thomas Ligotti Online, and Mike Davis's website, The Lovecraft eZine. Most articles which reported the controversy provided links to both Padgett and Davis's websites, likely increasing traffic to both websites.

In the short term, sales of Thomas Ligotti's books and awareness of his work have increased significantly.[45] The long-term impact of *True Detective*'s on Ligotti's work remains uncertain. Hopefully, increased awareness of his writing could lead to greater critical and academic study of Ligotti's work as well as sustained sales for the author, but only time will tell.

Thomas Ligotti and his publisher, Hippocampus Press, the only players in this drama with the legal right to make claims of copyright infringement and sue for damages, have chosen not to do so. They have also elected to remain silent. This silence likely indicates that Ligotti and his publisher have either agreed to a settlement with Pizzolatto / HBO, or that they are not interested in pursuing a case against Pizzolatto / HBO. While it does not answer all of the ethical questions around the use of Ligotti's work, this does answer the question of whether or not Pizzolatto should be branded a plagiarist. As creator of the work and rights holder, Thomas Ligotti and his publisher have the last word on that issue.

---

[45] VanderMeer, Jeff. "Thomas Ligotti 101: A Guide to the Cult Writer Now Linked to *True Detective*." Vulture. August 13, 2014. Accessed September 22, 2018. http://www.vulture.com/2014/08/thomas-ligotti-true-detective-guide.html#. "The media attention spiked sales of the book at the center of the controversy — Ligotti's nonfiction philosophy tome *The Conspiracy Against the Human Race* — to the point that it began to outsell Ayn Rand's *Atlas Shrugged*."

In the Groove: The Music of *True Detective*

The opening shot of episode seven, "After You've Gone," is a close-up view of a bar's jukebox. A row of records appears as black circles standing on their sides, displaying their concentric grooves and reinforcing the spiral motif which runs throughout *True Detective*. The camera stays on the jukebox until the needle drops, the record spins, and the first chords of a song begin to play. The music starts, preparing the audience, setting the mood before Hart and Cohle appear on screen and share a beer for the first time in over a decade. This shot serves as a subtle reminder that music is just as much a part of *True Detective* as the characters, plot, or literary references.

> The emotional communication between characters is enhanced by a very subtle score behind things.
> — Nic Pizzolatto

Musical accompaniment for a television show can be divided into two main components: the score and the source music. The score, or incidental music, is original music written specifically for the show. Often composed in collaboration with the director, the score sets the overall mood for the show, helps create atmosphere, and amplify the emotional impact of key scenes. Usually the score is comprised of ambient themes for individual characters, locations, events, or emotions. As the narrative of a show grows more complex, the themes can be combined to form new variations. Characters within a narrative typically do not hear the score of the show; it is an element of the story that exists only for the viewing audience.

Separate from the score, the source music is a set of songs that appear in a show as a result of action happening on screen, such as songs played at a party, by a D.J. at a bar, or on a car stereo. Characters within the narrative can be assumed to hear to the source music playing in the scenes where they appear. The source music is a part of the fictional world of the show and it usually features pre-recorded songs by a variety of artists. Using songs with established histories allow the musical director to play with an audience's associations with the musical genre, as a type of auditory shorthand to enhance a scene. The soundtrack of a show is all sound elements of a show combined: the score, source music, dialogue, background and sound effects.

The following appendix focuses on the source music for *True Detective*, but occasionally touches on other elements of the soundtrack. Readers should be aware that in the notes for each song, *only* the references or interpretations specifically attributed to T Bone Burnett or Nic Pizzolatto can be read as deliberately included by the creators of the show. Any other interpretations are made wholly by the author and in no way imply that these insights were intentional on the part of the creators.

Some of the songs in *True Detective* are played partially or at a very low volume, hindering a full experience of the music. Listening to the songs in full, separately from the soundtrack of the show is a rewarding exercise for *True Detective* fans who would like to fully immerse themselves into the rich sonic psychosphere crafted by T Bone Burnett.

> Your music is one of the main leads of this show and I consider it as essential a part of the vocabulary of *True Detective* as my writing.
> — Nic Pizzolatto, on T Bone Burnett's musical direction

Award winning musician/ producer T Bone Burnett composed the original score and selected the source music for *True Detective*. Burnett's impressive musical experience spans from playing guitar with Bob Dylan to crafting the soundtracks for *O Brother, Where Art Thou?*, *Walk the Line*, and *Inside Llewyn Davis*. In an interview included as a special feature on the *True Detective* Season 1 DVD / Blu-ray, Nic Pizzolatto called it "a huge plum" to land Burnett as musical director, indicating that they worked closely to craft a unique sound for the show. Wanting to avoid anything predictable or cliché, they aimed to create "a

Louisiana of the mind," with a soundtrack that "comes for from the psychology of the place rather than its exact musical history."[1] As a result, some of the songs included in *True Detective* may not be historically accurate for the time and location of the scenes in which they are used. The songs are, however, true to the emotions and experiences of the characters present in the scene.

In a 2014 interview with Mother Jones, Burnett explained that his musical choices for *True Detective* were driven by the characters, saying "The depth of character is the breadth of music you get to use. So all I have to do is imagine what they're listening to, and imagine the stories rattling around in their heads. How do you strengthen that? How do you make that resonate? It's about having the songs become part of the storytelling."[2] In multiple interviews, Burnett refers to reading the *True Detective* script for the first time as similar to reading a good novel, specifically a noir detective story. "I've always been interested in crime and true crime," he told *Mother Jones*. "If you listen to my records, like *Criminal Under My Own Hat*, you can feel it. I love Chandler and Hammett."[3] Burnett's passion shines through in the variety of songs he selected for *True Detective*, resulting in a soundtrack that does an amazing job of evoking the mindset of the characters, as well as the physical location of the story and the mood of the world in which the story takes place. This depth of character and breadth of musical selections make the *True Detective* soundtrack fertile ground for interpretation.

The Songs
Songs are listed by episode and in order of appearance within the episode.

Main Title Theme for *True Detective*
Song: Far from Any Road
Performed by: The Handsome Family
Notes: The Handsome Family's music is a mix of bluegrass, country and other American folk influences. Their song lyrics often tell the stories of murders both real and fictional. Their combination of macabre lyrics and menacing folk twang makes a perfect overture for *True Detective*, setting the proper mood for

---

[1] *True Detective* season 1. (2014). [DVD] Directed by F. Cary Joji. HBO Home Entertainment., "A Conversation with Nic Pizzolatto and T Bone Burnett," disc 3.
[2] Suebsaeng, Asawin. "T Bone Burnett on How He Chooses the Music for *True Detective*." Mother Jones. January 24, 2017. Accessed September 26, 2018. http://www.motherjones.com/mixed-media/2014/01/t-bone-burnett-true-detective-hbo-music-songs.
[3] Ibid.

enjoyment of a show that skirts the supernatural. The lyrics of "Far From Any Road" are filled with cryptic images of a poisoned land, blood, hunger, and stars in the night sky. In a March 2014 interview with the Washington Post, songwriter Rennie Sparks explained that the jimson weed plant was part of her inspiration for the song. "It's a plant that only blooms at night and you can see these huge white flowers and there are these moths that feed on them just at night so it's like a secret night time blooming and romance... there's a story of it driving people insane because it's psychedelic and because it gets into people's water all the time. So it's about these moths and this sexy, forbidden ritual they have in the darkness."[4] Madness, sex, compulsion and forbidden ritual appear in many forms throughout *True Detective*.

Episode 1: The Long Bright Dark

Song: Rocks and Gravel
Performed by: Bob Dylan
Scene: Detective Cohle questions prostitutes in truck stop bar
Notes: Included on the rare original pressings of Bob Dylan's 1963 album *The Freewheelin' Bob Dylan*, "Rocks and Gravel" was cut from subsequent pressings of the album by Columbia records. Unlike the rest of the songs on the album which are politically charged, "Rocks and Gravel" is a straightforward folk lament. The speaker of the song is a travelling man who needs "a good woman mama, to satisfy my weary soul."[5] This combination of song and scene suggests that the truck stop prostitutes Cohle interviews are petty criminals, but that they are also a part of the American tradition of wanderlust, travel, and life on the road. *True Detective* consistently mixes nostalgic or romantic ideas about small town America with the unpleasant reality that life in rural communities is just as corrupt and secretive as life in a big city.

Song: Sign of the Judgment
Performed by: The McIntosh County Shouters
Scene: Detectives Hart & Cohle drive to Marie Fontenot's house
Notes: Aside from the title theme, "Sign of the Judgment" is the only song used repeatedly in *True Detective* (see also episode 2: Seeing Things and episode 6: Haunted Houses). A driving gospel beat and apocalyptic lyrics complement the larger themes of the show, specifically the urgency of solving Dora Lange's murder and exposing the corruption at work in Vermilion Parish. A repeated verse mentions "Two tall angels, on a chariot wheel."[6] Considering that the song is often

---

[4] Lubitz, Rachel. "A Conversation with the Handsome Family, the Band Behind the *True Detective* Theme Song, 'Far from Any Road'." The Washington Post. March 05, 2014. Accessed September 26, 2018. http://www.washingtonpost.com/blogs/style-blog/wp/2014/03/05/a-conversation-with-the-handsome-family-the-band-behind-the-true-detective-theme-song-far-from-any-road/.

[5] Dylan, Bob. "Rocks and Gravel." *The Freewheeling Bob Dylan*. Columbia. 1963. MP3.

[6] The McIntosh County Shouters. "Sign of the Judgment." *Wade in the Water: African American Sacred Music Traditions Vol. I-IV*. Smithsonian Folkways Recordings. 1997. MP3

played while the detectives are in transit, the two angels could be Detectives Hart and Cohle, travelling through the bayou in their unmarked car, searching out the meaning behind mysterious signs and symbols.

Song: Young Men Dead
Performed by: The Black Angels
Scene: Cohle interview/ closing credits
Notes: The opening riff of this psychedelic rock piece plays over the end of the episode and the credits. The electric guitar serves as punctuation for Cohle's demand that Detectives Gilbough and Papina "start asking the right fuckin' questions."[7] When paired with Cohle's last line, the rebellious energy of "Young Men Dead" makes a compelling hook for the end of the first episode. Though the lyrics of the song do not come in until the credits are rolling, the song invites the listener to "pick up your feet and let's go,"[8] and join in a bloody fight. Though the audience may not realize it yet, they are about to accompany Detectives Cohle and Hart on a similarly difficult journey.

Episode 2: Seeing Things

Song: Unfriendly Woman
Performed by: John Lee Hooker
Scene: Detective Hart drinks in bar with fellow detectives
Notes: Blues legend John Lee Hooker's songs are quintessential bar music, ripe with moody guitar, buzzing harmonica, and lyrics that simultaneously celebrate and bemoan life's difficulties. "Unfriendly Woman" provides a bluesy atmosphere for Detective Hart's drinking and a hint that this episode will reveal his troubled relationships with women.

Song: One Bourbon, One Scotch, One Beer
Performed by: John Lee Hooker
Scene: Detective Hart calls his girlfriend, Lisa Tragnetti
Notes: Though it was not written specifically for him, Hooker's rendition of "One Burbon, One Scotch, One Beer" is one of the best known versions of the song and a perennial dive bar favorite. The lyrics include the lines, "I ain't seen my baby since night before last/ I wanna get drunk 'til I'm off of my mind."[9] Unlike the speaker in the song, Detective Hart is not content to drown his sorrows in alcohol and end the night alone. For Hart, drinking is what loosens his inhibitions, allowing him to call his girlfriend and seek physical satisfaction.

Song: Train Song
Performed by: Vashti Bunyan
Scene: Detective Hart and Lisa Tragnetti rendezvous

---

[7] *True Detective.* "The Long Bright Dark." Episode 1. Directed by Cary Joji Fukunaga. Written by Nic Pizzolatto. HBO. January 12, 2014.

[8] The Black Angels. "Young Men Dead." *Passover.* Blue Scholars / Light in the Attic. 2008. MP3.

[9] Hooker, John Lee. "One Bourbon, Once Scotch, One Beer." *The Real Folk Blues.* Chess Records. 1966. MP3.

Notes: Vashti Bunyan has been labelled as the godmother of "freak folk," a sub-genre which melds the acoustic instrumentation and universal themes of folk music with more avant-garde vocal styles and experimental narratives. Bunyan's high, bird-like voice is all that can be heard on "Train Song" in the scene between Detective Hart and Lisa Tragnetti. The sweetness of her voice lends a softness to the adulterous sex, a contrast to the handcuffs which Tragnetti uses on Hart. The lyrics tell the story of a woman travelling to meet an old lover, unsure if he will still be interested when her train arrives. The instability of the relationship described in the song matches the shaky connection shared by Tragnetti and Hart. The image of train tracks and the end of the line in the song creates a sense of inevitability for Tragnetti and Hart. Theirs is not a relationship with many possibilities – it is on a one-way track to a messy end.

Song: Sign of the Judgment
Performed by: The McIntosh County Shouters
Scene: Detective Cohle literally twists an arm to get directions to the "Hillbilly Bunny Ranch"
Notes: A few bars of "Sign of the Judgment" play over the scene where Cohle uses pressure to get directions out of the two previously uncooperative mechanics. The scene just before this is from the 2012 interview with Detective Hart, where he says of his partner, "Rust has about as sharp an eye for weakness as I ever seen."[10] These two scenes, back to back, with the inclusion of "Sign of the Judgment" tells viewers that Cohle passed judgment on the two mechanics, finding them weak willed enough that a little arm-twisting would make them talk.

Song: You Better Run to the City of Refuge
Performed by: Reverend C.J. Johnson
Scene: Detectives Hart and Cohle drive to the "Hillbilly Bunny Ranch" South of Spanish Lake
Notes: This song is a beautiful example of the power and energy of gospel music. Reverend Johnson's emphatic lead vocals are backed by his church choir and driven by double-time clapping during the verses. The song has many lyrical variations, most of which loosely relate to the biblical notion of "cities of refuge," places where people who committed manslaughter could seek refuge from blood vengeance sought by the families of their victims. Reverend Johnson's version of the song specifically mentions the city of Nineveh as the place to which people should run. In the bible, Nineveh was first regarded as a wicked city worthy of destruction. However, after Jonah preached to the Ninevites, they fasted and repented of their evil ways. God took mercy on them and their city because they had previously been ignorant of right and wrong. The Bunny Ranch can be read as a modern Nineveh, as the madam, Jan, informs Hart and Cohle that many of the girls living and working in the trailers have escaped from dangerous situations far worse than prostitution. The Bunny Ranch serves as a refuge because the girls have a place to live, protection from the law and their abusive families. Note that Dora Lange met a violent end after she left the refuge of the Bunny Ranch, not while she was living there.

---

[10] *True Detective*. "Seeing Things." Episode 2. Directed by Cary Joji Fukunaga. Written by Nic Pizzolatto. HBO. January 19, 2014.

Song: Meet Me in the Alleyway
Performed by: Steve Earle
Scene: Detective Cohle canvasses for Dora Lange sightings
Notes: The lyrics of "Meet Me in the Alleyway" tell the story of a man chasing the power of black magic, only to find that magic was part of his fate all along. "Can't run, can't hide from destiny" Earle drawls, "knew this day was callin' nearly all of my life."[11] When juxtaposed with Cohle canvassing for leads in the Dora Lange case, the song insinuates that Cohle is chasing something dangerous and magical, perhaps something he was fated to confront.

Song: If I Live or If I Die
Performed by: Cuff the Duke
Scene: Detectives Hart and Cohle drive to the abandoned church
Notes: This alt-country song pleads to the lord for truth and answers, but the line "My faith is weary, my soul is too/ Lord if you hear me, I need some proof"[12] fits well with the situation Hart and Cohle find themselves in when they go to investigate the abandoned church. They are at a weak point in their investigation, with few leads that could lead them to the truth of who murdered Dora Lange. They are reduced to hunches and driving around in circles looking for abandoned churches. The "Anti-Christian Crimes Task Force" is hot to take over the Dora Lange investigation and the Detectives need some proof that they are on the killer's trail in order to keep control of the case. Just when the detectives believe the burned-out church is yet another dead end, Cohle watches a flock of birds and hallucinates that they form a spiral before flying away. This vision is a sign of sorts, a proof to Cohle that the church is vital to their investigation. His hunch is rewarded when the detectives investigate the interior of the church and find the killer's telltale artwork and symbols, thus keeping the investigation alive.

Song: Kingdom of Heaven
Performed by: The 13th Floor Elevators
Scene: Detectives Hart and Cohle discover mural in abandoned church
Notes: Psychedelic rock provides the perfect accent to the closing scene of an episode entitled, "Seeing Things." Detectives Hart and Cohle are literally seeing a mural most likely painted by Dora's killer. The lyrics to "The Kingdom of Heaven" are an ominous mix of the religious imagery of stained glass and incense with lyrics about transformation. The song includes the line, "it bathes you with its glory and you begin life anew."[13] In context of the scene, the song feels as if it is a conversation between the killer and his victim. The speaker of the song sees reverence and glory in the sacrifice he is about to make, an unleashing of the victim's potential, rather than a gruesome death.

---

[11] Earl, Steve. "Meet Me in the Alleyway." *I'll Never Get Out of This World Alive.* New West Records. 2011. MP3.

[12] Cuff the Duke. "If I Live or if I Die." *Sidelines of the City.* Hardwood Records. 2007. MP3.

[13] 13th Floor Elevators. "Kingdom of Heaven." *The Psychedelic Sounds of the 13th Floor Elevators.* Charly. 2002. MP3.

Episode 3: The Locked Room

Song: Stand by Me
Performed by: The Staple Singers
Scene: Detectives Hart and Cohle attend Friends of Christ tent revival
Notes: The use of gospel tracks in *True Detective* provides a counterpoint for Detective Cohle's anti-religious diatribes and general distain for people who turn to religion in times of need. Gospel music focuses on the struggles of mankind, on people in mortal and spiritual crisis who cry out to God because they have been abused and forsaken by their fellow man. These people are vulnerable, just as Dora Lange was when she visited the tent revival. They make easy prey for predatory preachers, false prophets, or worse. The lyrics of "Stand by Me" plead "Thou who never lost a battle/ Stand by me."[14] Dora Lange may not have found the help she needed from religion, but Detectives Hart and Cohle provide the next best thing; they stand by her and the case for two decades until the killer is brought to justice.

Song: Does My Ring Burn Your Finger
Performed by: Buddy Miller
Scene: Rust arrives at Longhorn's bar for double date
Notes: All of the songs that play during the Detectives' double date in Longhorn's fall in the Country & Western genre, adding to the barn dance atmosphere of the bar, along with the bales of hay and the old-fashioned lanterns on the table. The choice of genre also highlights detective Hart's troubled romantic life, which casts a cloud over the evening. "Does My Ring Burn Your Finger" draws attention to Maggie's growing doubts about her marriage. The lyrics "Did my ring burn your finger?/ Did my love weigh you down?/ Was the promise too much to keep around?"[15] are the lament of a faithful spouse trying to understand why love wasn't enough to hold a marriage together.

Song: I'm a One Woman Man
Performed by: Johnny Horton
Scene: Detective Hart joins Lisa Tragnetti at the bar
Notes: The country twang of Johnny Horton's guitar is almost all that can be heard of "I'm a One Woman Man" in the scene, but the few lyrics that do float through are enough for the viewer to know that the song is a darkly humorous jab at Detective Hart's infidelity. The man is on a date with his wife, but leaves her at the table to chase after his girlfriend, while the lines "I'll always love you honey and I'll never let you down/ I'll never love another, even if I can/ Oh, come to me baby, I'm a one woman man"[16] fill the air.

Song: The Heart That You Own
Performed by: Jo-El Sonnier (Credited as Jo Ell Sonnier)
Scene: first song of dance scene at Longhorn's bar

---

[14] The Staples Singers. "Stand by Me." *Swing Low*. MNR Media. 2011. MP3.

[15] Miller, Buddy. "Does My Ring Burn Your Finger?" *Cruel Moon*. Shout! 2014. MP3.

[16] Horton, Johnny. "I'm a One Woman Man." *Honky Tonk Man: The Essential Johnny Horton 1956-1960*. Columbia/ Legacy. 1996. MP3.

Notes: "The Heart That You Own" was originally a Dwight Yoakam song, but it's covered by a live band in the scene at Longhorn's bar. The members of the band are not actors, but real musicians. The accordion player is Jo-El Sonnier, who is best known for his Cajun music. Having a live band cover a song that was playing on Country radio in 1995 is a subtle but effective way to remind the audience of both the time and place of this flashback scene. As with all the other songs in the scene, "The Heart That You Own" is relevant to detective Hart's marriage. The speaker in the song laments "used to be I could love here for free/ way back before you bought the property/ now I pay daily on what once was mine."[17] Both Maggie and Marty Hart are constrained by the effort it takes to maintain their relationship. The date night, which should be a chance to reconnect and remember why they fell in love, comes across more like a chore, a payment they must make in order to keep their marriage alive.

Song: Evangeline Special
Performed by: Jo-El Sonnier (Credited as Jo Ell Sonnier)
Scene: second song of dance scene at Longhorn's bar
Notes: "Evangeline Special" is old-time Cajun music performed by the legendary Jo-El Sonnier and features a lengthy accordion solo. The joyful energy of the song makes a stark contrast with the less than festive moods of the detectives as they dance with their partners.

Episode 4: Who Goes There

Song: Bring It to Jerome
Performed by: Bo Diddley
Scene: Detectives canvass for leads
Notes: The titular Jerome is likely Jerome Green, Bo Diddley's maracas player and co-vocalist on the song. Bo Diddley's signature beat and lack of chord changes create a mood of anticipation. The listener waits for a harmonic build and release of tension, but the song remains on a single chord throughout, creating an insistent drone and offering no release. The unresolved tension and rocking rhythm of the song parallel the mood of the detectives as they question all manner of local characters, searching for any information that might give them a lead. It also highlights their need to "bring home" the case – to find a suspect before the Anti-Christian Crimes Task Force takes over the investigation.

Song: Illegal Business
Performed by: KRS One/ Boogie Down Productions
Scene: Stripper dances in American flag costume
Notes: In the interview included as a special feature on the *True Detective* box set, T Bone Burnett and Nic Pizzolatto[18] address the choice of using a politically-conscious hip hop song as the soundtrack for a scene set in a Louisiana strip club.

[17] *True Detective.* "The Locked Room." Episode 3. Directed by Cary Joji Fukunaga. Written by Nic Pizzolatto. HBO. January 26, 2014.
[18] Watch for Nic Pizzolatto's cameo in the strip club scene. He is the bartender wearing a shirt that reads "Kiss me I'm an asshole." In interviews, Pizzolatto mentions that he previously worked in Louisiana strip clubs, so his cameo may be a winking reference to his pre-Hollywood employment.

They both acknowledge that it was unlikely that a D.J. in a predominantly white, Southern strip club would play this song, but point out that the music of *True Detective* was not meant to be historically accurate. Burnett notes that the music was meant to be more evocative of mood and character. He explains his choice by saying, "It was the right song to play in that scene. We tried a lot of songs to play in that scene, but when that one went in there everyone said 'Oh! There it is.' It's appropriate for *True Detective* in 2014 and the story we're telling."[19]

Part of what makes "Illegal Business" appropriate for the strip club scene are the lyrics, which focus on corrupt cops who profit off the war on drugs. As KRS-One raps his lyrics expose the hypocrisy of a police force that claims to be acting for the good of the people, but in reality is just as deeply invested with the drug trade as any dealer or addict. As the chorus says, "Cocaine business controls America/ Ganja business controls America."[20] The song provides an important point of contrast. For all their personal failings, Detectives Hart and Cohle are not corrupt in the way that the cops in "Illegal Business" are corrupt. They seek no personal profit from their contact with the drug world. They only want the information necessary to stop a killer. Additionally, the song echoes Cohle's past undercover work with the drug task force and foreshadows his return to using his undercover identity.

Song: The Brain Center at Whipple's
Performed by: The Melvins
Scene: Warehouse rave where Tyrone reveals the whereabouts of Reggie Ledoux
Notes: The sound of this Melvin's alt metal track provides a primal and foreboding accompaniment to Detective Hart's walk through the flashing lights and spark showers of the rave. The lyrics to the song, however, are unintelligible in the scene. Only the base line and a few guitar riffs carry through chaos, mirroring Hart's disorientation in the unfamiliar environment.

Song: Sur Le Borde de L'Eau (On the Water's Edge)
Performed by: Blind Uncle Gaspard
Scene: Bar where Detective Cohle shares his plan to revive his undercover identity[21]

---

[19] *True Detective* season 1. (2014). [DVD] Directed by F. Cary Joji. HBO Home Entertainment., "A Conversation with Nic Pizzolatto and T Bone Burnett," disc 3.
[20] KRS One/ Boogie Down Productions. "Illegal Business." *By All Means Necessary*. Jive/ RCA Records. 1998. MP3.
[21] Set design in *True Detective* is one of the elements which makes multiple viewings of the show rewarding. In a blink-and-you'll-miss-it shot of the bar where Cohle shares his plan to revive his undercover identity, we see that all the barstools have mannequin legs attached to the seats and extending down to the ground. This creates the illusion that everyone seated at the bar is really standing, but that their lower halves are comically mismatched with their upper halves. Cohle is seated at a stool featuring what appears to be a woman's bare legs and voluptuous backside covered only by a thong bikini. It's a quick bit of visual humor, but also a nod to the exploration of Cohle's split identity.

Notes: This 1929 recording of a Cajun song is a rare find. Sung in Creole French, it is a variation on a series of traditional French songs that tell the story of an innocent girl who is lured aboard a ship by a wicked captain. In some versions of the song, the girl escapes through cunning and bravery, but in this version the girl is not so lucky. In this version of the song, she comes to a gruesome end. The narrative of the song echoes the tragic fates of missing women and children in the Louisiana bayou, while providing a subtle background for Hart and Cohle's important conversation.

Song: Are You Alright?
Performed by: Lucinda Williams
Scene: Detective Cohle prepares for undercover work
Notes: This plaintive folk-rock tune has been featured in the soundtrack of several shows and movies, largely due to the intimacy and urgency present in Lucinda Williams's voice as she repeats the titular question again and again. Like the speaker in the song, Detectives Hart and Cohle are questioning themselves, and each other, as their lives spiral out of control.

Song: Rainin' in My Heart
Performed by: Slim Harpo
Scene: Detective Cohle and Maggie meet in a diner to discuss her separation from Detective Hart
Notes: The swamp-blues classic "Rainin' in My Heart" is a tidy summation of where Maggie and Marty's troubled marriage stands. The speaker of the song is a lover pleading for another chance. "You got me cryin'/ 'Bout to lose my mind/ Don't let me cry in vain/ Try my love just once, again."[22] The lyrics of the song mirror Marty's plea to Maggie. Marty is not physically present in the scene, but Cohle is there on his behalf, trying to persuade Maggie to reunite with her husband. Just as the song is faint in the background, Cohle's attempt to plead Hart's case is overshadowed by Maggie's disgust and anger.

Song: A History of Bad Men
Performed by: The Melvins
Scene: Detective Cohle enters biker bar as "Crash"
Notes: Featuring an experimental sound and dark, offbeat humor of the music of the Melvins is a good fit for Cohle's entrance to the biker bar. Cohle is trying on his old "Crash" identity and there is a certain dark humor to the idea that he is impersonating a previous version of himself. The title of the song echoes Cohle's earlier assertion that he and Detective Hart are "bad men."[23] In this scene, Cohle is literally at the door of a nest of bad men and being accepted as one of their own. Lyrically, the chorus emphasizes the perilous nature of Cohle's mission, calling attention to the fact Cohle is acting as a mole. "Did you hear that, I got a real bad

[22] Harpo, Slim. "Rainin' in My Heart." *Slim Harpo Sings "Raining in My Heart."* Excello Records. 1961. MP3.
[23] *True Detective.* "The Locked Room." Episode 3. Directed by Cary Joji Fukunaga. Written by Nic Pizzolatto. HBO. January 26, 2014.

feeling.../ How many moles do you suppose they're keeping?"[24] The line, "Don't make a sound they're not dead, just sleeping" emphasizes that Cohle's connection to his "Crash" persona is still strong. The lyric is mirrored when Cohle, speaking as "Crash" asks, "Do I look dead, motherfucker?"[25]

Song: American Life
Performed by: Primus
Scene: Detective Hart attempts to enters biker bar
Notes: Known for their irreverent alt-metal sound, Primus gets serious with the lyrics of "American Life." The song has no chorus, only three verses that draw thumbnail sketches of how different individuals strive for the American dream but are left unfulfilled: an Italian immigrant landing on Ellis Island, a Laotian refugee eking out a living on minimum wage, and a homeless veteran who supports himself by digging through trash for cans to recycle. This song points to the dirty underbelly of the dream and it is significant that it plays while Hart is on screen. Initially, detective Hart seems to embody the American Dream – a successful job, beautiful wife, happy children, and spacious home – but in truth, Hart is close to losing everything he holds dear.

Song: Holy Mountain
Performed by: Sleep
Scene: Detective Cohle boards a boat with Ginger and the Iron Crusaders
Notes: "Holy Mountain" first appeared on the seminal stoner metal album of the same name. At nearly nine minutes long, the song is a drone of power chords and doom, setting an ominous mood as detective Cohle descends into the drug-fueled criminal underworld of the Iron Crusaders.

Song: Clan in da Front
Performed by: Wu-Tang Clan
Scene: Iron Crusaders invade the Hoston stash house
Notes: A cut from the influential East Coast hip-hop album *Enter the Wu-Tang (36 Chambers)*, this song provides a gritty accompaniment to the action inside the Hoston project stash house. "Clan in da Front's" minimalist sound in no way detracts from its power. The starkness of the beat and the vocals draw attention to the violent themes in the lyrics. The song begins with a mad litany of over 25 names/ identities of the Wu-Tang Clan members, conjuring the image of a large group of performers. This abundance of names and bodies is in keeping with the crowded and claustrophobic environment of the stash house. Additionally, the repeated line "Wu-Tang Killa Beez, we on a swarm"[26] echoes the chaotic buzz of voices in the stash house, where no one voice is clear and no reason can come to the fore. The anger and confusion in the room is palpable and soon to explode in exactly the kind of violence described in the Wu-Tang's lyrics.

---

[24] The Melvins. "A History of Bad Men." *A Senile Animal*. Ipecac Recordings. 2006. MP3.

[25] *True Detective*. "The Locked Room." Episode 3. Directed by Cary Joji Fukunaga. Written by Nic Pizzolatto. HBO. January 26, 2014.

[26] Wu-Tang Clan. "Clan in da Front." *Enter the Wu-Tang Clan (36 Chambers)*. RCA Records. 2013. MP3.

Song: Honey Bee (Let's Fly to Mars)
Performed by: Grinderman
Scene: end of six-minute tracking shot (overhead helicopter view)
Notes: Hard rocking "Honey Bee" opens with a frenzied wall of sound, dominated by a siren-like electric guitar riff that perfectly matches the energy and danger of Cohle's run through the Hoston projects. The song starts just as the perspective on the action switches from eye level to an overhead shot from the point of view of a police helicopter. This shift broadens the field of view for the audience, allowing them to see the labyrinthine streets of the projects flood with agitated residents and cops responding with guns drawn. The shot provides an ominous sense that the Iron Crusaders raid on the stash-house is just the spark that could light the dry tinder bed of the projects into a conflagration of violence and death.

Episode 5: The Secret Fate of All Life

Song: Casey's Last Ride
Performed by: Kris Kristofferson
Scene: Detective Cohle and Ginger meet Reggie Ledoux in the Sportsman bar
Notes: Country legend Kris Kristofferson's love of literature comes through in his songs, which often feature strong narrative elements. "Casey's Last Ride" tells the story of a lonely married man riding the subway and dawdling at a bar before going home. Written in a minor key and with a plodding beat, the song has a foreboding sound appropriate to the feelings of trepidation that both Ginger and Cohle must have as they sit at the bar waiting for Reggie Ledoux. The opening lyrics are an eerie take on the quotidian act of descending into the subway, likening it to death and descent into the underworld. "Casey joins the hollow sound of silent people walking down/ The stairway to the subway in the shadows down below... The poison air he's breathin' has the dirty smell of dying."[27] This juxtaposition of the mundane and the uncanny parallels the conversation between Cohle and Reggie. Cohle tries to pursue a drug deal, but Reggie refuses on the grounds that he dislikes Cohle, telling him, "I can see your soul at the edges of your eyes. It's corrosive, like acid. You got a demon, little man."[28] Both the conversation and the song are a hint that there's something odd and otherworldly behind the murders in the bayou.

Song: Tired of Waiting for You
Performed by: The Kinks
Scene: Detective Hart tries to reconcile with Maggie at roller rink
Notes: One of the Kinks early and more pop-influenced songs, "Tired of Waiting for You" evokes the melancholy of a troubled relationship. The song plays as Detective Hart tries to convince Maggie that he has changed enough for her to take him back. There is a sense of hopelessness to the conversation between the two characters. The audience is left with the feeling that nothing is truly resolved between them, but that they will inevitably get back together and repeat their mistakes again and again. The scene visually reinforces the sense of repetition with roller skaters endlessly circling the rink, while the lyrics of the song drone on

---

[27] Kristofferson, Kris. "Casey's Last Ride." *Kristofferson*. Monument. 1970. MP3.

[28] *True Detective*. "The Secret Fate of All Life." Episode 5. Directed by Cary Joji Fukunaga. Written by Nic Pizzolatto. HBO. February 16, 2014.

the same refrain, "I was a lonely soul/ I had nobody till I met you/ But you keep-a me waiting/ All of the time/ What can I do?"[29]

Song: Eli
Performed by: Bosnian Rainbows
Scene: Detective Cohle inspects devil catchers in an abandoned school
Notes: "Eli'" hovers somewhere between psych rock and industrial. The steady base line turns the refrain "Why do you smile at me?"[30] into an enigmatic question. The song, like the scene, has a dream-like quality. Both Cohle and the speaker of the song are remembering past events, questioning what they thought they knew and finding no answers.

Episode 6: Haunted Houses

Song: Waymore's Blues
Performed by: Waylon Jennings
Scene: Detective Hart drinks at the Fox and the Hound[31] bar
Notes: The loping beat of this country tune makes it a perfect drinking song for Detective Hart when he stops off at the Fox and Hound after running errands for his wife and daughters. Waylon Jennings's lyrics are an apt expression of Hart's romantic problems and bad omen for his ability to stay faithful to his wife. "Well, I got a good woman, what's the matter with me?/ What makes me want to love every woman I see?"[32] When Hart is joined by Beth, who reveals herself as one of the girls from the "Hillbilly Bunny Ranch" from episode two, the song spells out Hart's inevitable infidelity. "I was trifling when I met her now I'm trifling again."[33]

Song: Les Champs Élysée
Performed by: Bobby Charles
Scene: Detective Hart and Beth smoke in front of a bar
Notes: Sung in French, "Les Champs Élysée," is a traditional song showcasing the stylistic versatility of swamp-pop pioneer Bobby Charles. Everything about the song evokes the mood of a Paris café on a summer evening, from the lilting accordion to the graceful piano to the gentle, yet passionate vocals. This is a soundtrack for falling in love, which makes the contrast between the song and the scene all the more striking. Beth and detective Hart are not sipping wine at a Paris café; they are smoking cigarettes in the parking lot of a roadside bar. Beth and Hart are both seeking something, but what they find in each other is not the romantic love of "Les Champs Élysée."

---

[29] The Kinks. "So Tired of Waiting for You." *Kinda Kinks*. Pye/ Reprise. 1965.MP3.
[30] Bosnian Rainbows. "Eli." *Bosnian Rainbows*. Clouds Hill/ Sargent House. 2013. MP3.
[31] The Fox and The Hound is a popular name for bars and pubs, but it also makes a fitting description of *True Detective*'s lead characters. Rust Cohle is the wild and wily, quick-witted fox, while Marty Hart is the domesticated, hard-working hound, who is also a dog when it comes to how he treats women.
[32] Jennings, Waylon. "Waymore's Blues." *Dreaming My Dreams*. RCA Victor. 1975. MP3.
[33] Ibid.

Song: Every Man Needs a Companion
Performed by: Father John Misty
Scene: sex scene between Beth and Detective Hart
Notes: An indie rock blend of piano, mandolin and tambourine create a folksy framework for a duet of sorts between Father John Misty's (a.k.a. J. Tillman of the Fleet Foxes) warm, open lead vocals and the harmonizing of the female backing singers. The speaker's longing is palpable in the lines "Every man needs a companion/ Someone to console him/ Someone like you,"[34] while the chorus of women's voices agrees, soothes, and affirms. Like the speaker in the song, Detective Hart has a deep-rooted need for companionship. Though he fills the need with extramarital sex, his needs are not only physical, they are also emotional. Beth regards Hart as a good man because of his concern for her welfare when she was an underage prostitute at the "Hillbilly Bunny Ranch," and a hero for his bravery in raiding the Ledoux compound. Desperate to escape his tension in his work life and his ruined marriage at home, Hart is eager for the companionship of someone who sees him in such a favorable light.

Song: Variations Goldberg, BWV 988 Aria
Performed by: Glenn Gould
Scene: Detective Cohle visits Kelly, the catatonic girl rescued from the Ledoux compound
Notes: The only piece of classical music to appear in *True Detective*, the "Variations Goldberg" was written by Johan Sebastian Bach. Comprised of thirty variations and an aria, it is an impressive example of how a single musical theme can be adapted to create new variations that are both related to the original and yet still unique. The piece begins with the aria, the baseline of which serves as the theme upon which all the following movements elaborate. Only the aria plays in the scene where Detective Cohle visits Kelly in a psychiatric care facility. Classical piano seems an obvious choice of music for calming disturbed psychiatric patients; however, the form and structure of "Variations Goldberg" lend it a greater significance to the scene. In the seven years since she was rescued from the Ledoux compound, Kelly has been catatonic. Her entire consciousness is trapped in a "locked room,"[35] where she is forced to live her horrific experience over and over. Her life has become a sick version of the "Goldberg Variations," an ever more baroque and obsessive meditation on the unspeakable abuse that is the defining theme of her life. When Detective Cohle visits her, he asks Kelly to return to the locked room, the starting point of her trauma, just as the aria, the starting point of the Goldberg Variations, plays in the background.

Song: The Good Book
Performed by: Emmylou Harris
Scene: Maggie Hart meets a stranger at a bar
Notes: This country-infused folk song highlights the hypocrisy of men using religion as a justification for their destructive behavior, with the lines "Well, it's a shame/

---

[34] Misty, Father John. "Every Man Needs a Companion." *Fear Fun*. Bella Union. 2012. MP3.
[35] *True Detective*. "The Locked Room." Episode 3. Directed by Cary Joji Fukunaga. Written by Nic Pizzolatto. HBO. January 26, 2014.

How could so much evil be done/ In the Good Book's name?"[36] Although that sentiment is relevant to the theme of corruption that runs throughout *True Detective*, the song also speaks to Maggie's unspoken frustration with the traditional family values to which she has held true, but that her husband violates. Emmylou Harris's strong sweet voice asks, "Oh God, how can you / Be so cruel? / And let men name you and claim you / And use you as a tool?"[37] In context of Maggie's situation, the "you" in these lyrics can be read as Maggie questioning herself and her actions. Maggie is fed up with her marriage and realizing that she has allowed herself to be named and claimed as Marty Hart's wife, used as mother of his children and source of his comfort and stability, while getting very little satisfaction in return for her fidelity.

Song: Too Many Tears in My Eyes
Performed by: Ike & Tina Turner
Scene: Cohle receives a visit from Maggie
Notes: The intensity and emotion of Tina Turner's voice in this rock tune echoes Detective Cohle's internal conflict, as he drinks alone in his apartment and reviews a sprawling collage of evidence around unsolved murders and missing persons. Though he has been formally suspended from the police department, Cohle continues to work the case because he is emotionally invested in it, just as the speaker in the song is emotionally invested in a man who is marrying someone else. Unable to rally departmental support to investigate the cases further, Cohle shines his flashlight on the pictures of missing and murdered women, numbing his heart and clouding his mind with alcohol. The lyrics "There were too many tears in my eyes/ there was too much pain in my heart/ I just had to let the teardrops start"[38] emphasize that Cohle is already overwhelmed with his own pain and emotion before Maggie arrives at his doorstep in tears.

Song: Core Chant
Performed by: Meredith Monk
Scene: Rust Cohle and Maggie Hart sex scene
Notes: This minimalist piece features wordless vocals accompanied only by the percussive notes of a marimba. The song's focus on the voice as a tonal instrument rather than vehicle for language lends an atavistic feeling to Cohle and Maggie's sex. They strip themselves of their clothes, their words, responsibilities, and social boundaries. At the moment of their coupling, they expose their most core selves, as well as their raw need for connection and release. "Core Chant" is one part of the score for *Mercy*, an avante-garde musical theater performance which Meredith Monk describes as "a meditation on the human capacity to both extend and withhold compassion, kindness, empathy, and mercy."[39] The emotional

---

[36] Harris, Emmylou. "The Good Book." *The Inner Flame*. Fire Records. 2012. MP3.
[37] Ibid.
[38] Turner, Ike & Tina. "Too Many Tears in My Eyes." *Put on Your Tights Pants*. Soul Vibes. 1999. MP3.
[39] "Creative Capital." Creative Capital - Investing in Artists Who Shape the Future. Accessed September 26, 2018. http://www.creative-capital.org/index.php?url=projects/view/248.

complexity of this piece suits the tangle of ill-defined emotions Maggie and Cohle experience before, during, and after their sexual encounter.

Song: Sign of the Judgment
Performed by: Cassandra Wilson
Scene: closing credits
Notes: The third use of the song in *True Detective* (see episode one, "The Long Bright Dark" and episode two, "Seeing Things") was recorded specially for the show and is a much slower and less exuberant version than what is used in earlier episodes. Cassandra Wilson's soulful timbre adds a reflective air to this version of "Sign of the Judgment." This change is appropriate, as the detectives are much older men at his point in the story and are making their first wary contact in years. Bringing back the song just as Cohle and Hart reunite is symbolically significant as well. It played when they began their first investigation of the marshland cult killings – the first lap around the spiral and it plays again as they return to the case to repay their debt – their second rotation on spiral. Repeating "Sign of the Judgment" is a sign that the story has looped and begun a new iteration of the same pattern.

Episode 7: After You've Gone
Song: Angel of the Morning
Performed by: Juice Newton
Scene: Bar where Marty Hart and Rust Cohle reunite[40]
Notes: The penultimate episode of *True Detective* begins with a shot of a beautiful old jukebox. The camera closes in to show the mechanics of the album cards flipping to Juice Newton's 1981 pop album *Juice* before the record sets and spins. The image of a round record with concentric groves is a visual reminder that the story is resetting and that the characters are beginning a fresh lap around the same track. In "Angel of the Morning" Juice Newton's sweet, strident voice insists she is ready to spend the night with a man with no strings attached. This act of faith mirrors the faith that Hart and Cohle must put in each other when they talk about reopening old cases and old wounds. The song also foreshadows the darkness and light metaphor used in the closing of the final episode with lyrics, "If we're victims of the night/ I won't be blinded by the light" and "I'm old enough to face the dawn."[41] As older, wiser men, Hart and Cohle are finally ready to face the real darkness that awaits them in Errol's Carcosa and still be able to find light at the end of the harrowing journey.

Song: Trance Figure
Performed by: School of Seven Bells
Scene: Rust Cohle interviews Tobey Boelert a.k.a Johnny Joannie

---

[40] Note that a few bars of the McIntosh County Shouters version of "Sign of the Judgment" plays as the camera closes in on the jukebox, before "Angel of the Morning" begins. This snippet may be included just to give a sense of continuity between episodes, as the Cassandra Wilson version of "Sign of the Judgment" closed the previous episode.
[41] Newton, Juice. "Angel of the Morning." *The Best of Juice Newton*. Vanguard. 2005.MP3.

Notes: The electronically modified and mechanically precise vocals of "Trance Figure" create a disorienting, ethereal feel to the dream pop track, making it an apt choice for Cohle's conversation with gender-bending Johnny Joannie. A former classmate of Marie Fontenot at one of the Tuttle-funded religious schools, Johnny Joannie claims not to remember anything, but will discuss his memories of abuse under the guise that they are dreams. The lyrics of "Trance Figure" echo Johnny Joannie's memories of fantasy blurring with reality, yet never resolving into something comprehensible. Cohle's investigation has led him to the edge of reality, a place where stories of half-remembered men with burns and animal faces are his best chance at finding a killer.

Song: Floating Bridge
Performed by: Gregg Allman
Scene: Rust Cohle introduces Marty Hart to the owner of the Doumain's Domain
Notes: The high-stepping honky-tonk instrumental of "Floating Bridge" can barely be heard in the background of this scene, but Gregg Allman's twang comes through between lines of dialogue before Cohle introduces his boss, Robert Doumain. The song tells the story of a man who almost drowns while hiding under a floating bridge. The lyrics make it clear that this experience was an important event in the speaker's life, repeating the line "Well, I never will forget that floatin' bridge"[42] six times. Cohle is more succinct in explaining the defining incident in his boss's life, saying only, "Bob had a little boy, been missing since '85."[43]

Song: Red Light
Performed by: Vincent and Mr. Green (featuring Ravenbird)
Scene: Marty Hart and Rust Cohle travel to Miss Delores interview
Notes: "Red Light" provides a blend of hip-hop and smoky cabaret vocals as Hart and Cohle walk into a crowded housing block to interview a former Tuttle family domestic worker, Miss Delores. The song has a carnival atmosphere, echoing a barker's cry with the lyrics "Red light stop/ Green light go/ Where she lands/ No one knows."[44] Hart and Cohle are taking a gamble in interviewing Miss Delores. She is a tired old woman and they have no way of knowing if the information she gives them will be useful or accurate. Their conversation with her stops and starts before circling back around to the strange and ominous Carcosa mentioned in Dora Lange's diary.

Song: Fault Line
Performed by: Black Rebel Motorcycle Club (BRMC)
Scene: Marty Hart and Rust Cohle discuss their former boss, Steve Geraci
Notes: From BRMC's folk and blues inspired album *Howl*, "Fault Line" features a rolling melody laid atop crisp acoustic guitar. The combination of voice, guitar and harmonica usually evoke a relaxed, back-porch atmosphere, but "Fault Line" has an

---

[42] Allman, Gregg. "Floating Bridge." *Low Country Blues*. Rounder Records. 2011. MP3.

[43] *True Detective*. "After You've Gone." Episode 7. Directed by Cary Joji Fukunaga. Written by Nic Pizzolatto. HBO. March 2, 2014.

[44] Vincent & Mr. Green (featuring Ravenbird). "Red Light." *Vincent & Mr. Green*. Ipecac Recordings. 2004. MP3.

air of the dramatic as well. The refrain "Racin' with the risin' tide to my father's door"[45] conveys a sense of imminent disaster. At this point in the story, Hart and Cohle have uncovered information that their old boss, Steve Geraci, may have been involved in hushing up the Marie Fontenot case. Unlike Hart and Cohle, Geraci is still an active member of the police force. When Hart and Cohle start asking him questions about old cases, they call attention to themselves and to their investigation, setting in motion a race to solve the marshland cult killings before the corrupt police department can shut them down.

Song: Did She Jump or Was She Pushed?
Performed by: Richard and Linda Thompson
Scene: Maggie visits Cohle at Doumain's Domain
Notes: Recorded while the husband and wife rock duo Richard and Linda Thompson's marriage was crumbling, "Did She Jump or Was She Pushed?" is a simple arrangement supporting a complex thematic mix of mystery and doubt. The circumstances around the song's recording make it an easy metaphor for the attempt to place blame after a failed relationship. In *True Detective*, the song plays as Cohle looks up from his work at the bar to see Maggie pull into the parking lot. Cohle watches Maggie not directly, but through a reflection in the mirror behind the bar, reminding the viewer that Cohle isn't just reacting to seeing Maggie for the first time in years; he is also reflecting on their past and why she chose to seduce him. Cohle's face remains impassive as the lyrics play. "She crossed a lot of people/ Some she called friends."[46] Was Maggie forced to use infidelity as a tool to exit her marriage, to make Hart let her go, or did she choose to seduce Cohle out of spite, knowing it would hurt both men equally? The line "Did she jump or was she pushed?" highlights the core question about Maggie's infidelity. Maggie's actions ended her marriage, but depending on how a viewer interprets it, she either jumped out of the marriage of her own volition or was pushed out by Hart's serial cheating and chronic inattention to his family.

The refrain "Did She Jump or Was She Pushed?" is also relevant to the larger mystery of *True Detective*. The lines, "They found some fingerprints/ Right around her throat/ They didn't find no killer/ And they didn't find no note"[47] outlines the problem with investigating the missing women and children of the bayou. They are a marginalized population, impoverished, itinerant and oftentimes engaged in high-risk behaviors like prostitution and drug use. Rather than untangle the messy web of intentional disappearances, accidental deaths, and possible murders, the Louisiana police choose the most convenient answers, supporting corruption and a murder cult through garden-variety incompetence and laziness.

Song: Lungs
Performed by: Townes Van Zandt
Scene: view of river and cemetery with Errol mowing a lawn[48] and closing credits

---

[45] Black Rebel Motorcycle Club. "Fault Lines." *Howl*. ECHO. 2005. MP3.

[46] Thompson, Richard & Linda. "Did She Jump or was She Pushed?" *Shoot Out the Lights*. Hannibal Records. 1982. MP3.

[47] Ibid.

[48] Note that Errol mows the grass of the cemetery in a spiral pattern.

Notes: This haunting mining ballad is written from the point of view of a man trapped underground, awaiting his inevitable death by asphyxiation. The lyrics move from pleading for aid "Won't you lend your lungs to me?/ Mine are collapsing," to morbid, and finally to apocalyptic with "Fill sky with screams and cries/ Bathe in fiery answers."[49] The only percussion in the song is the knock of Van Zandt's knuckle against the wood of his guitar, empty as the thump of a coffin lid. "Lungs" is a song of the soon to be deceased, those for whom death is a stark and personal reality. Appropriately, the song starts to play just as the camera pulls away from Errol Childress to reveal the long rows of white marble vaults of the cemetery behind him, hinting at his familiarity with death. Once Errol is revealed as the man with the scars, *True Detective* moves into its final phase, where death will take center stage.

Episode 8: Form and Void

Song: The Angry River
Performed by: The Hat, featuring Father John Misty & S. I. Istwa
Scene: closing credits
Notes: Aside from the score and the song Errol whistles to himself, "The Angry River" is the only song to appear in the final episode of *True Detective* and was written by T Bone Burnett expressly as the closing song for the season. In the interview included as a special feature on the *True Detective* DVD/ Blu-ray, Burnett and Nic Pizzolatto discuss how the song came about. Burnett explained that the lyrics came "out of our discussions about the show and the country and the story we were telling... this music grew out of the score really, this theme, the main theme to *True Detective*. It grew out of that and the psychosphere theme we had."[50] From the lilting violin to the muted chorus of female voices, the song is suffused with a sense of melancholy. The lyrics remind the listener of "the bitter taste the hidden face/ of the lost forgotten child," as well as the "awful cost of all we lost/ as we looked the other way."[51] This is a song about unreconciled debts, loss and the constant struggle of life, "The angry river rises/ As we step into the rain."[52] These last lines of the song mirror the last scene of the show: Hart and Cohle walking into the night together. Their story does not end with stasis. It ends with catharsis and forward momentum.

Bonus Tracks

Songs not listed as part of the official HBO soundtrack.

Song: Clear Spot
Performed by: Captain Beefheart (a.k.a. Don Van Vliet)
Scene: N/A– mentioned in interviews, does not appear on rebroadcast or DVD/ Blu-ray

---

[49] Van Zandt, Townes. "Lungs." *Townes Van Zandt*. Poppy. 1969. MP3.

[50] *True Detective* season 1. (2014). [DVD] Directed by F. Cary Joji. HBO Home Entertainment., "A Conversation with Nic Pizzolatto and T Bone Burnett," disc 3.

[51] *True Detective*. "Form and Void." Episode 8. Directed by Cary Joji Fukunaga. Written by Nic Pizzolatto. HBO. March 9, 2014.

[52] Ibid.

Notes: In several interviews, including his conversation with *Mother Jones*, T Bone Burnett mentioned that he selected the song "Clear Spot" by Captain Beefheart for use in a scene where detective Cohle sifts through photographic evidence. The song is not listed on the official HBO *True Detective* website and does not appear in any of the HBO streaming versions or the DVD/Blue-ray. Even if the song did not make it into the permanent recording of *True Detective*, it is worth discussing. T Bone Burnett felt the song gave viewers a clue about what Cohle might be thinking or feeling while obsessively reviewing the details of a case. "He's alone in a room, and he's looking at photographs of dead women — what kind of music is he listening to?" Burnett said in the Mother Jones interview, "...well, he's not going to be listening to music about his truck, or music about how tight his jeans are, or music about how much beer he's had to drink before he gets in the truck. He's gonna be listening to some Captain Beefheart."[53]

Known for its innovative mix of jazz, blues, rock, and classical, Captain Beefheart's music is influential, but has never gained mainstream success. Including Beefheart in Cohle's collection is a subtle insight into his character. Over the course of the show, the viewer does not get a good look into Cohle's interests outside of detective work, drinking, and pessimist philosophy, but knowing that he is someone who appreciates the complex and quirky music of Beefheart hints at a deeper interest in experimental music and arts.

Though it is not straight Louisiana-style blues or Southern rock, "Clear Spot" evokes the sticky, claustrophobic feeling of summer in the bayou. It features a swampy guitar, a baseline that sounds as if it was blown on an empty moonshine jug and Beefheart's vocals buzzing like cicadas. Lyrically, it highlights the natural menace of the swamp, including lines like "Mosquitos 'n moccasins steppin' all around/ 'fraid I'm gonna get hit/ I have to run so far to find a clear spot."[54] The juxtaposition of these lyrics with Cohle's obsession with evidence photos of murdered women hints that Cohle is thinking not just about the way that these women died, but also about how they lived – that they were running from danger, afraid, and ultimately unable to find the safety of a clear spot before they became victims of the killer lurking in the bayou.

Song: The Kingdom of Gold (possible)
Written by: Mark Knopfler
Scenes: Whistled by Errol leaving his daddy's cabin and while working at the school
Notes: The final episode of *True Detective* gives a view into the daily life of Errol Childress. While at home and at work, he whistles a tune. The ostensibly innocent act of whistling becomes creepy when juxtaposed with Errol's degenerate world of incest and murder. NY Mag interviewed Glenn Fleshler, the actor who played Errol Childress, about the preparation he did for the role. "I did a lot of watching of the

---

[53] Suebsaeng, Asawin. "T Bone Burnett on How He Chooses the Music for *True Detective*." Mother Jones. January 24, 2017. Accessed September 26, 2018. http://www.motherjones.com/mixed-media/2014/01/t-bone-burnett-true-detective-hbo-music-songs.
[54] Captain Beefheart & His Magic Band. "Clear Spot." *Clear Spot*. Reprise Recoreds. 1972. MP3.

Andy Griffith shows, which were referenced in the original script,"[55] said Fleshler. The two shows have very little in common other than both being set in the rural South, but there's one small similarity: whistling. *The Andy Griffith Show* features an opening wherein the affable sheriff Taylor whistles a pleasant tune while walking to the local fishing hole with his young son. Given that Fleshler watched episodes of *The Andy Griffith Show* as preparation for the role of Errol Childress, perhaps he chose to whistle a tune in a twisted imitation of the 1960's television show.

The song which Errol whistles is not identified in the episode credits, nor is it listed on the official HBO *True Detective* website. Neither Nic Pizzolatto nor T Bone Burnett have mentioned it in interviews. The enigmatic source of the song has been the subject of much online debate, with speculation ranging from the upbeat "My Favorite Things" from *Sound of Music* to "Ievan Polkka," a Finnish Polka. The author prefers to believe that Errol is whistling the spooky folk-rock tune "Kingdom of Gold" by former Dire Straits front man Mark Knopfler. The melody is a loose fit (as are any of the other potential matches listed here), but the lyrics of the Knopfler song echo imagery associated with *True Detective*'s Yellow King cult and Errol's beliefs that he is soon to ascend beyond the "disc and loop"[56] of mortal life. The lyrics in "Kingdom of Gold" tell of a "high priest of money" presiding over a corrupted city which prays to "the gods of the bought and the sold." The song also tells of a "pack of dog jackals" which arrive to threaten the Kingdom of Gold, but which will be conquered by the priest king's "axes and armor" before being hung "in the wind from his citadel walls."[57] Additionally, the narrative in "City of Gold" matches the finale of *True Detective*. Errol, as a priest of the Yellow King attempts to defend his skeleton-strewn citadel from the invading forces of Cohle and Hart.

---

[55] Herzog, Kenny. "*True Detective*'s Glenn Fleshler on Playing Lawn-Mowing Monster Errol Childress." Vulture. March 10, 2014. Accessed September 26, 2018. http://www.vulture.com/2014/03/true-detective-errol-childress-glenn-fleshler-interview.html.

[56] *True Detective*. "Form and Void." Episode 8. Directed by Cary Joji Fukunaga. Written by Nic Pizzolatto. HBO. March 9, 2014.

[57] Knopfler, Mark. "Kingdom of Gold." *Privateering*. 2012. Mercury Records. 2012. MP3.

Not Everyone Wants to Sit Alone in an Empty Room Beating Off to Murder Manuals: Recommended Reading

The following list was compiled by the author, with the generous help of Adam Stewart and Mark Stewart, authors of Appendix 1, "The Guide to *True Detective* and Weird Comic Book Fiction," as well as Miguel Rodriguez, Founder of the Horrible Imaginings Film Festival and Podcast.[1] The suggestions below are pulled from the film noir, hardboiled detective, cosmic horror, and Southern gothic genres. The non-fiction selections include philosophical essays, scientific works, and documentaries.

Fiction

Barker, Clive. *The Hellbound Heart.* New York: Harper, 2007.

Barron, Laird. *The Imago Sequence and Other Stories.* San Francisco: Night Shades, 2009.

Bierce, Ambrose. *Ambrose Bierce: The Devils Dictionary, Tales, & Memoirs.* New York, NY: Literary Classics of the United States, 2011.

---

[1] hifilmfest.com.

Blackwood, Algernon. *Ancient Sorceries and Other Weird Stories*. Edited by S. T. Joshi. New York, NY: Penguin Books, 2002.

Bolaño, Roberto. *2666: A Novel*. London: Picador, 2009.

Campbell, John W. *Who Goes There?*. Edited by William F. Nolan. Somerset, PA: Rocket Ride Books, 2009.

Campbell, Ramsey. *The Grin of the Dark*. New York: Tom Doherty Associates, 2008.

Cardin, Matt. *Divinations of the Deep*. Ashcroft, B.C.: New Century Macabre, an Imprint of Ash-Tree Press, 2002.

Carr, Caleb. *The Alienist*. New York: Random House, 1994.

Chambers, Robert W. *The King in Yellow*. New York, NY: Fall River Press, 2014. [*The King in Yellow* is in the public domain. eBook files are available to download for free at via the Gutenberg project. http://www.gutenberg.org/ebooks/8492.]

Chandler, Raymond. *The Big Sleep*. New York: Vintage Crime, 1996.

Conrad, Joseph. *Heart of Darkness*. Newburyport: Dover Publications, 2012.

Danielewski, Mark Z. *House of Leaves*. New York: Pantheon Books, 2000.

Dick, Philip K. *VALIS*. Boston: Mariner Books, 2011.

Eco, Umberto. *The Name of the Rose*. Translated by William Weaver. Boston: Mariner Books, Houghton Mifflin Harcourt, 2014.

Ellroy, James. *L.A. Confidential*. New York: Warner Books, 1997.

Evenson, Brian. *Last Days: A Novel*. Minneapolis: Coffee House Press, 2016.

Faulkner, William. *Santuary: The Corrected Text*. New York: Vintage, 1993.

Faulkner, William. *As I Lay Dying*. Modern Library, 2000.

Franklin, Tom. *Smonk*. New York: Harper Perennial, 2007.

Gay, William. *Twilight: A Novel*. Ann Arbor, MI: Dzanc Books, 2016.

Hine, Phil. *The Pseudonomicon*. Original Falcon Press, 2009.

Hodgson, William Hope. *The House on the Borderland*. London: Penguin, 2008.

Hawthorne, Nathaniel. *Young Goodman Brown and Other Tales*. Oxford: Oxford University Press, 1998.

Julavits, Heidi. *The Vanishers*. New York: Anchor, 2013.

Kiernan, Caitlín R. *Threshold: A Novel of Deep Time*. New York: Roc, 2001.

Klein, T. E. D. *Dark Gods: Four Tales*. Toronto: Bantam Books, 1986.

Laidlaw, Marc. *The 37th Mandala*. New York City: Leisure Books, 1999.

Lansdale, Joe R. *The Drive-In: A Double-Feature Omnibus*. New York: Carroll & Graf, 1997.

Ligotti, Thomas. *Teatro Grottesco*. London: Virgin Books, 2008.

Ligotti, Thomas, and Jeff VanderMeer (forward). *Songs of a Dead Dreamer and Grimscribe*. Penguin Classics, 2015.

Lovecraft, H. P. *Tales of the Cthulhu Mythos*. New York: Del Rey, 1998.

Machen, Arthur, S. T. Joshi (introduction), and Guillermo Del Toro (forward). *The White People and Other Weird Stories*. Penguin Books, 2011.

McCarthy, Cormac. *Child of God*. London: Picador, 2010.

Pessl, Marisha. *Night Film: A Novel*. New York: Random House Trade Paperbacks, 2014.

O'Connor, Flannery. *The Violent Bear It Away*. New York: Farrar, Straus & Giroux, 2007.

Pizzolatto, Nic. *Between Here and the Yellow Sea*. Ann Arbor, MI: Dzanc Books, 2015.

Pizzolatto, Nic. *Galveston: A Novel*. New York: Scribner, 2011.

Smith, Clark Ashton, and S. T. Joshi (introduction). *The Dark Eidolon and Other Fantasies*. NY, NY: Penguin Books, 2014.

Southern, Terry. *The Magic Christian.* NightHawk Books, 2015.
Wagner, Karl Edward. *In a Lonely Place.* Santa Cruz, CA: Scream/Press, 1984.
Woolrich, Cornell. *Night Has a Thousand Eyes.* New York: Ballantine, 1983.
VanderMeer, Jeff. *Area X: The Southern Reach Trilogy.* New York: Farrar, Straus and Giroux, 2014.

Nonfiction

Blackmore, Susan J. *The Meme Machine.* Oxford: Oxford University Press, 2000.
Burton, Dan, and David Grandy. *Magic, Mystery and Science: The Occult in Western Civilization.* Bloomington, IN: Indiana University Press, 2004.
Cioren, E.M. *A Short History of Decay,* Penguin Books, 2018.
Cioran, E. M. *The Temptation to Exist.* Translated by Richard Howard. Chicago: University of Chicago Press, 1998.
Conrad, Mark T (ed.). *The Philosophy of Film Noir.* Lexington: University Press of Kentucky, 2007.
Covington, Dennis. *Salvation on Sand Mountain: Snake Handling and Redemption in Southern Appalachia.* Cambridge, MA: Da Capo Press, 2009.
Davenport-Hines, R. P. T. *Gothic: 400 Years of Excess, Horror, Evil, and Ruin.* New York: North Point Press, 1999.
Eco, Umberto. *From the Tree to the Labyrinth: Historical Studies on the Sign and Interpretation.* Translated by Anthony Oldcorn. Cambridge: Harvard University Press, 2014.
Eco, Umberto. *Semiotics and the Philosophy of Language.* Bloomington: Indiana University Press, 1986.
Hawking, Stephen, and Leonard Mlodinow. *The Grand Design.* Random House USA, 2012.
Hirsch, Foster. *The Dark Side of the Screen: Film Noir.* Cambridge, MA: Da Capo Press, 2008.
Hite, Kenneth. *Tour De Lovecraft: The Tales.* Alexandria, VA: Atomic Overmind Press, 2008.
Ligotti, Thomas. *The Conspiracy against the Human Race a Contrivance of Horror.* New York: Hippocampus, 2010.
Kaku, Michio. *Hyperspace: A Scientific Odyssey through Parallel Universes, Time Warps, and the Tenth Dimension.* New York: Anchor Books, 1995.
Kern, Hermann. *Through the Labyrinth: Designs and Meanings over 5,000 Years.* Munich: Prestel, 2000.
King, Stephen. *Danse Macabre.* New York: Gallery, 2010.
Nietzsche, Friedrich Wilhelm. *Thus Spoke Zarathustra: A Book for All and None.* Pantianos Classics, 2017.
Place, Janey. "Women in Film Noir." In *Women in Film Noir.* London: British Film Institute, 1998.
Royle, Nicholas. *The Uncanny.* Manchester: Manchester University Press, 2008.
Thacker, Eugene. *In the Dust of This Planet: Horror of Philosophy [Vol. 1].* Zero Books, 2011.
Thacker, Eugene. *Starry Speculative Corpse: Horror of Philosophy [Vol 2].* Zero Books, 2015.
Thacker, Eugene. *Tentacles Longer Than Night: Horror of Philosophy [Vol. 3].* Zero Books, 2015.
Zapffe, Peter Wessel. "The Last Messiah." *Philosophy Now,* March/April 2004.

Comics/ Graphic Novels

Brubaker, Ed. *Fatale volumes 1 -5.* Image Comics. 2014-2015.
Ligotti, Thomas. *The Nightmare Factory volumes 1 - 2.* Fox Atomic. 2007.
Mignola, Mike *Hellboy volumes 1 – 13.* Dark Horse Comics. 1993 – ongoing.
Moore, Alan. *From Hell (collected edition).* Top Shelf Productions. 1999
Moore, Alan. *Watchmen (collected edition).* DC Comics. 1987.
Moore, Alan. *Neonomicon (collected edition). Avatar Press. 2011.*
Moore, Alan. *Top 10 (collected edition).* Vertigo. 2015.
Morrison, Grant. *The Invisibles volumes 1 -3.* Vertigo 1994-2000.
Morrison, Grant. *Seven Soldiers: Mister Miracle issues 1 – 4.* DC Comics. 2005-2006.
Morrison, Grant. *The Mystery Play.* Vertigo. 1994.
Van Lente, Fred. *Weird Detective (collected edition).* Dark Horse Books. 2017.

Film

AM 1200. Directed by David Priot. 20018.
Blue Velvet. Directed by David Lynch. 1986.
Big Lebowski. Directed by Joel and Ethan Coen. 1998.
Chinatown. Directed by Roman Polanski. 1974.
Dagon. Directed by Stuart Gordon. 2001.
Dead Man's Shoes. Directed by Shane Meadows. 2004.
Double Indemnity. Directed by Billy Wilder. 1944.
Europa Report. Directed by Sebastián Cordero. 2013.
Event Horizon. Directed by Paul W. S. Anderson. 1997.
From Beyond. Directed by Stuart Gordon. 1986.
Grant Morrison: Talking with Gods. Directed by Patrick Meaney. 2010.
Hush, Hush Sweet Charlotte. Directed by Robert Aldrich. 1964.
In the Mouth of Madness. Directed by John Carpenter. 1994.
Marshland (La Isla Minima). Directed by Alberto Rodríguez. 2014.
Memories of Murder (Salinui Chueok). Directed by Bong Joon-ho. 2003.
Mildred Pierce. Directed by Michael Curtiz. 1945.
Mud. Directed by Jeff Nichols. 2012.
Night and the City. Directed by Jules Dassin. 1950.
Night of the Hunter. Directed by Charles Laughton. 1955.
Pontypool. Directed by Bruce McDonald. 2008.
Swamp Water. Directed by Jean Renoir and Irving Pichel.1941.
The Beyond (E tu Vivrai nel Terrore! L'aldilà). Directed by Lucio Fulci. 1981.
The Call of Cthulhu. Directed by Andrew Leman. 2005.
The Lady from Shanghai. Directed by Orson Welles.1947.
The Mindscape of Alan Moore. Directed by Dez Vylenz. 2003.
The Thing. Directed by John Carpenter. 1982.
The Secret in Their Eyes (El Secreto de Sus Ojos). Directed by Juan José Campanella. 2009.
The Third Man. Directed by Carol Reed. 1949.
Wise Blood. John Huston. 1979.

Websites/ Online Resources

http://darknessbecomesyou.com/. Official HBO website.
http://wekeeptheotherbadmenfromthedoor.com/. Graphic tribute to *True Detective.*

http://www.vulture.com/2014/03/true-detective-glossary.html. Glossary of all
    names, places and things in *True Detective*, season 1.

http://kinginyellow.wikia.com. The Yellow Site, a wiki for everything associated with
    Robert W. Chambers's Yellow Mythos.

http://www.ligotti.net/. Created by fans, a homepage for horror writer Thomas
    Ligotti. News, online stories, forum, downloads.

http://lovecraftzine.com/. A magazine featuring weird fiction, cosmic horror, and
    the Cthulhu mythos.

Thanks for the Beer: Acknowledgements

There are many people who deserve thanks for helping bring this book to fruition. The first thank you goes to everyone at the Sequart Organization for offering me the opportunity to publish these essays. Special thanks are due to my editor, Mike Phillips, for his guidance, enthusiasm, and patience.

Thank you to the Tuesday night writer's group: Elaine Smith, Amanda Hutchins Gogatz, Kelly Arndell, Wes Warner, and Aseret Sperry. Your commentary made this a better book, but more importantly, your humor kept me sane.

Thank you to my publishing colleagues, Andy Albrecht, Brenna Wood, and Jeff Rossetti. Your support helped me manage my career while still finding time to write.

Thank you to my parents, Jeff and Sally Turner, for encouraging me and for exposing me to so much wonderful film, music, art, and literature. Thanks as well to my sister, Christine Turner, for being my partner in crime on clandestine library trips and late-night movie marathons.

Lastly, thank you to my husband Tone Milazzo, who first encouraged me to write these essays. This book wouldn't exist without you.

About the Author

Melissa Milazzo works in scientific publishing but is neither a rocket scientist nor a brain surgeon. Since 2001 she has managed journals, developed reference works, wrangled authors, and partnered with researchers to improve the discoverability of scientific information.

Melissa lives in San Diego, California with her novelist husband and two illiterate dogs. *Time is a Flat Circle: Examining True Detective, Season 1* is her first book.

ALSO FROM **SEQUART**

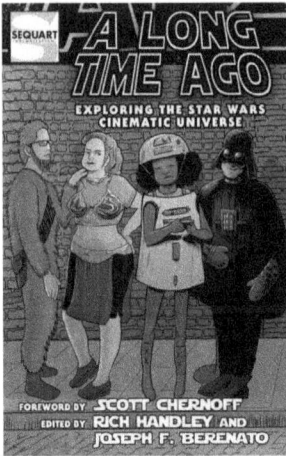

A LONG TIME AGO: EXPLORING THE STAR WARS CINEMATIC UNIVERSE
A GALAXY FAR, FAR AWAY: EXPLORING STAR WARS COMICS
A MORE CIVILIZED AGE: EXPLORING THE STAR WARS EXPANDED UNIVERSE

SOMEWHERE BEYOND THE HEAVENS: EXPLORING BATTLESTAR GALACTICA
NEW LIFE AND NEW CIVILIZATIONS: EXPLORING STAR TREK COMICS
BRIGHT LIGHTS, APE CITY: EXAMINING THE PLANET OF THE APES MYTHOS

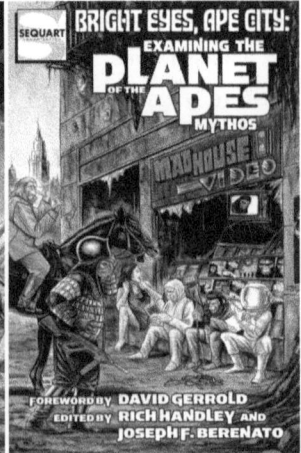

BOOKS ON GRANT MORRISON:

GRANT MORRISON: THE EARLY YEARS

OUR SENTENCE IS UP: SEEING GRANT MORRISON'S *THE INVISIBLES*

CURING THE POSTMODERN BLUES: READING GRANT MORRISON AND CHRIS WESTON'S *THE FILTH* IN THE 21ST CENTURY

THE ANATOMY OF ZUR-EN-ARRH: UNDERSTANDING GRANT MORRISON'S BATMAN

BOOKS ON WARREN ELLIS:

SHOT IN THE FACE: A SAVAGE JOURNEY TO THE HEART OF *TRANSMETROPOLITAN*

KEEPING THE WORLD STRANGE: A *PLANETARY* GUIDE

VOYAGE IN NOISE: WARREN ELLIS AND THE DEMISE OF WESTERN CIVILIZATION

WARREN ELLIS: THE CAPTURED GHOSTS INTERVIEWS

OTHER BOOKS:

THE CYBERPUNK NEXUS: EXPLORING THE BLADE RUNNER UNIVERSE

THE SACRED SCROLLS: COMICS ON THE PLANET OF THE APES

THE BRITISH INVASION: ALAN MOORE, NEIL GAIMAN, GRANT MORRISON, AND THE INVENTION OF THE MODERN COMIC BOOK WRITER

HUMANS AND PARAGONS: ESSAYS ON SUPER-HERO JUSTICE

CLASSICS ON INFINITE EARTHS: THE JUSTICE LEAGUE AND DC CROSSOVER CANON

MOVING TARGET: THE HISTORY AND EVOLUTION OF GREEN ARROW

THE DEVIL IS IN THE DETAILS: EXAMINING MATT MURDOCK AND DAREDEVIL

TEENAGERS FROM THE FUTURE: ESSAYS ON THE LEGION OF SUPER-HEROES

THE BEST THERE IS AT WHAT HE DOES: EXAMINING CHRIS CLAREMONT'S X-MEN

AND THE UNIVERSE SO BIG: UNDERSTANDING *BATMAN: THE KILLING JOKE*

MINUTES TO MIDNIGHT: TWELVE ESSAYS ON *WATCHMEN*

THE WEIRDEST SCI-FI COMIC EVER MADE: UNDERSTANDING JACK KIRBY'S *2001: A SPACE ODYSSEY*

WHEN MANGA CAME TO AMERICA: SUPER-HERO REVISIONISM IN *MAI, THE PSYCHIC GIRL*

THE FUTURE OF COMICS, THE FUTURE OF MEN: MATT FRACTION'S *CASANOVA*

MOVING PANELS: TRANSLATING COMICS TO FILM

MUTANT CINEMA: THE X-MEN TRILOGY FROM COMICS TO SCREEN

GOTHAM CITY 14 MILES: 14 ESSAYS ON WHY THE 1960S BATMAN TV SERIES MATTERS

IMPROVING THE FOUNDATIONS: *BATMAN BEGINS* FROM COMICS TO SCREEN

DOCUMENTARY FILMS:

DIAGRAM FOR DELINQUENTS

SHE MAKES COMICS

THE IMAGE REVOLUTION

NEIL GAIMAN: DREAM DANGEROUSLY

GRANT MORRISON: TALKING WITH GODS

WARREN ELLIS: CAPTURED GHOSTS

COMICS IN FOCUS: CHRIS CLAREMONT'S X-MEN

For more information and for exclusive content, visit Sequart.org.

www.ingramcontent.com/pod-product-compliance
Lightning Source LLC
Chambersburg PA
CBHW021230090426
42740CB00006B/461